ALGAR TRAVEL GUIDE

2024

Discover the Hidden Gems, Must-See Attractions and Local Insight of Portugal's Southern Gem

Phil Curtis

All rights reserved. No part of this book may be reproduced, stored in a retrieval system, or transmitted in any form or by any means, electronic, mechanical, photocopying, recording, or otherwise, without the prior written permission of the copyright owner. The information contained in this book is for general information purposes only. The author and publisher make no representations or warranties of any kind, express or implied, about the completeness, accuracy, reliability, suitability or availability with respect to the book or the information, products, services, or related graphics contained in the book for any purpose. Any reliance you place on such information is therefore strictly at your own risk.

Copyright © 2024 by Phil Curtis.

TABLE OF CONTENT

Introduction ———————————————— 7
    About the Region ————————————— 8
    Best Time to Visit —————————————— 9
    Getting There and Around ———————— 11

Attractions ——————————————————— 15
    Beaches ————————————————————— 15
    Historic Sites ————————————————— 18

Restaurants —————————————————— 23
    Seafood Specialties ————————————— 23
    Traditional Portuguese Cuisine ————— 26
    International Dining ————————————— 34
    Budget Eats ———————————————————— 36
    Fine Dining Experiences ——————————— 38

Hidden Gems —————————————————— 41
    Off-the-Beaten-Path Villages ——————— 41
    Local Markets and Artisan Shops ———— 45
    Secret Beaches and Coves ————————— 48
    Quaint Cafés and Bars ———————————— 50
    Cultural Festivals and Events ——————— 53

Accommodation ————————————————— 63
    Luxury Resorts ———————————————— 63
    Boutique Hotels ——————————————— 66
    Budget Hostels ——————————————— 69
    Vacation Rentals —————————————— 72

- Eco-Friendly Lodgings — 74

Outdoor Activities — 79
- Surfing and Watersports — 79
- Hiking Trails — 82
- Golf Courses — 85
- Boat Tours and Sailing — 87
- Horseback Riding — 91

Nightlife and Entertainment — 97
- Beach Bars and Clubs — 97
- Live Music Venues — 99
- Traditional Fado Houses — 103
- Casino and Gaming — 106

Practical Information — 111
- Currency and Payment Methods — 111
- Language and Communication — 114
- Safety Tips — 116
- Local Customs and Etiquette — 118

Resources — 123
- Transportation Guide — 123
- Recommended Websites and Apps — 125

Conclusion — 129
- Final Tips and Recommendations — 129
- Share Your Experience — 130
- Farewell to Algarve — 132

BONUS SECTION — 135

Itinerary Suggestions _____ **135**
  Outdoor Adventure Itinerary _____ 135
  Romantic itinerary _____ 140
  Coastal itinerary _____ 144
  Budget friendly itinerary _____ 148
  Historical itinerary _____ 154
  Art and culture itinerary _____ 160
  Gastronomic Adventure _____ 163
  Nature and Parks Day _____ 166
  Music and Nightlife Excursion _____ 171
  Family friendly itinerary _____ 174
Custom Travel Journal _____ **177**

DISCLAIMER!!!

Welcome to my Algarve Travel Guide. We appreciate your choice in selecting our guide for your travel needs. It is important to note that this guide intentionally does not include images or maps, and we would like to provide clarity on this decision.

In crafting Algarve Travel Guide, our primary focus was on delivering a streamlined, immersive, and distraction-free reading experience. By omitting images and maps, we aimed to encourage readers to engage more deeply with the descriptive narrative and cultivate a mental image of the destinations. We believe that this approach allows for a more personal connection with the information provided, fostering a unique and subjective experience for each reader.

Furthermore, the decision to exclude images and maps is rooted in our commitment to environmental sustainability. Printing high-quality images can contribute significantly to the environmental footprint of a publication. By choosing a text-only format, we hope to reduce our impact on the environment and encourage eco-conscious travel practices.

We understand that visual aids are valuable for some travelers, and we encourage readers to use complementary resources, such as online maps or travel apps, in conjunction with this guide for a comprehensive travel experience.

Thank you for choosing my Algarve Travel Guide. We hope you find the absence of images and maps enhances your reading experience, allowing you to immerse yourself fully in the rich narrative of your upcoming journey.

Safe travels!

SCAN QR CODE TO SEE MAP OF ALGARVE

Introduction

Welcome to the Algarve, where the sun-kissed shores meet the azure waters of the Atlantic Ocean in a harmonious dance of beauty and relaxation. Nestled in the southernmost region of Portugal, the Algarve beckons travelers with its irresistible blend of stunning landscapes, rich history, and vibrant culture.

As you step foot into this enchanting region, you'll find yourself surrounded by a tapestry of colors - from the golden sands of its pristine beaches to the verdant greenery of its rolling hills. The Algarve is a paradise for nature lovers, boasting a diverse range of ecosystems that are home to a myriad of plant and animal species.

But it's not just the natural beauty that captivates visitors; the Algarve is also steeped in history and culture, with ancient castles, Moorish architecture, and quaint villages waiting to be explored. Whether you're wandering through the narrow cobblestone streets of historic towns like Silves or admiring the intricate tilework of centuries-old churches, each corner of the Algarve tells a story of its rich heritage.

And then there are the beaches - the crown jewels of the Algarve. With over 150 kilometers of coastline to explore, you'll be spoiled for choice when it comes to finding your slice of paradise. From secluded coves and hidden bays to bustling resort towns and lively beach bars, there's a beach for every mood and occasion in the Algarve.

But the Algarve isn't just about sunbathing and swimming; it's also a haven for outdoor enthusiasts. Whether you're an adrenaline junkie looking to catch some waves on one of the region's world-class surf spots or a hiker seeking out breathtaking views along the rugged coastal trails, the Algarve offers endless opportunities for adventure and exploration.

Of course, no trip to the Algarve would be complete without indulging in its world-renowned cuisine. From freshly caught seafood and succulent grilled meats to hearty stews and sweet pastries, the Algarve's culinary scene is a feast for the senses. Be sure to sample local specialties like grilled sardines, cataplana (a traditional seafood stew), and pastéis de nata (custard tarts) for a true taste of the region.

And when the sun sets, the Algarve comes alive with a vibrant nightlife scene. Whether you're sipping cocktails at a beachfront bar, dancing the night away at a bustling nightclub, or enjoying a traditional fado performance in a cozy tavern, there's no shortage of ways to keep the party going after dark.

So welcome to the Algarve, where every moment is an opportunity for adventure, relaxation, and discovery. Whether you're here to soak up the sun on its pristine beaches, immerse yourself in its rich history and culture, or simply indulge in its delicious cuisine, the Algarve is sure to capture your heart and leave you longing to return again and again.

About the Region

Algarve, a name that rolls off the tongue like a whispered secret, holds within its borders a tapestry of landscapes that weave together seamlessly. From the dramatic cliffs of Ponta da Piedade to the pristine beaches of Praia da Marinha, each corner of this coastal paradise tells a story of its own.

The heart of Algarve beats with a rhythm that is as vibrant as it is laid-back. Here, time seems to slow down, allowing visitors to savor every moment of their stay. Whether you're seeking relaxation on sun-kissed shores or adventure amidst rugged terrain, Algarve has something to offer for every traveler.

As the gateway to the Atlantic, Algarve has been shaped by centuries of maritime history and cultural exchange. Phoenician, Roman, and Moorish influences can be seen in the architecture, cuisine, and traditions that permeate the region. From the ancient walls of Silves to the bustling markets of Loulé, traces of the past are woven into the fabric of everyday life.

But Algarve is more than just a destination; it's a state of mind. It's the feeling of warm sand between your toes, the taste of freshly caught seafood, and the sound of waves crashing against the shore. It's a place where strangers become friends over glasses of vinho verde, and where every sunset feels like a gift from the gods.

In the following pages, we invite you to embark on a journey of discovery through Algarve's most treasured sights and hidden gems. From the sun-drenched beaches to the charming hillside villages, let us be your guide as we uncover the magic of this coastal paradise together. Welcome to Algarve, where every moment is a memory in the making.

Best Time to Visit

Let me take you on a journey through the sights, sounds, and flavors of the Algarve, starting with the best time to visit.

The Algarve is a destination that boasts year-round appeal, each season offering its own unique charm. However, there are certain times of the year when the region truly shines, making it an ideal time for travelers to experience its wonders to the fullest.

Spring (March to May):
As the winter chill fades away, the Algarve bursts into life with the arrival of spring. This is a time when nature awakens from its slumber, blanketing the countryside in a riot of color. The weather is mild and pleasant, with temperatures gradually rising as the season progresses. Spring is perfect for outdoor adventures such as hiking along coastal trails or exploring the region's lush countryside. It's also a great time to visit historic sites and charming villages without the crowds that flock to the Algarve during the peak summer months.

Summer (June to August):
Summer is undoubtedly the most popular time to visit the Algarve, and for good reason. With long days of sunshine and warm temperatures, it's the perfect time to soak up the sun on the region's stunning beaches. Whether you're looking for secluded coves or lively resort towns, the Algarve has a beach to suit every taste. Summer also brings a vibrant atmosphere to the region, with festivals, concerts, and cultural events taking place throughout the summer months. From seafood festivals to traditional fado performances, there's always something happening in the Algarve during the summer.

Autumn (September to November):
As the summer crowds disperse and the temperatures begin to cool, autumn is a wonderful time to visit the Algarve. The weather remains warm and pleasant, making it ideal for outdoor activities such as golfing, hiking, and exploring the region's natural beauty. Autumn is also harvest season in the Algarve, with vineyards and orchards laden with ripe fruit waiting to be picked. Visitors can sample the region's delicious wines and local delicacies at food festivals and wine tastings held throughout the autumn months.

Winter (December to February):
While the Algarve may not be the first destination that comes to mind for a winter getaway, it has plenty to offer visitors during the colder months. With mild temperatures and fewer tourists, winter is a great time to explore the region's historic sites, museums, and cultural attractions without the crowds. The Algarve's golf courses are also in full swing during the winter months, attracting golf enthusiasts from around the world. And if you're craving some winter sun, the Algarve's beaches are still beautiful at this time of year, perfect for a leisurely stroll or a brisk dip in the sea.

Getting There and Around

As you prepare to embark on your journey to the sun-kissed shores of the Algarve, you'll find a myriad of transportation options available to suit your preferences and budget. Whether you're arriving from across the globe or neighboring regions, accessing this picturesque paradise is a breeze.

Arriving in Algarve

By Air:
The quickest and most convenient way to reach the Algarve is by air. Faro Airport (FAO) serves as the main gateway to the region, welcoming flights from major cities across Europe and beyond. Airlines such as TAP Portugal, Ryanair, and easyJet offer regular connections to Faro Airport, ensuring accessibility from various international destinations.

Upon arrival at Faro Airport, you'll find an array of transportation options to take you to your final destination within the Algarve. Taxis are readily available outside the terminal, offering a convenient door-to-door service to hotels and resorts. Alternatively, car rental companies operate from the airport, providing the flexibility to explore the region at your own pace.

By Train:
For travelers seeking a scenic journey to the Algarve, arriving by train is an excellent option. Portugal's national railway company, Comboios de Portugal (CP), operates regular services connecting major cities like Lisbon and Porto to the Algarve. The Alfa Pendular and Intercidades trains offer comfortable and efficient travel, with stops at key destinations including Faro, Lagos, and Portimão.

The train journey from Lisbon to Faro typically takes around 3 hours, offering passengers breathtaking views of the Portuguese countryside along the way. Once you arrive at your chosen station, taxis and local buses are available to transport you to your accommodation or desired attractions.

By Road:
Driving to the Algarve provides travelers with the freedom to explore the region's stunning landscapes at their own pace. Portugal boasts a well-maintained network of highways, making road travel a convenient option for visitors arriving from neighboring countries.

From Lisbon, the journey to Faro by car takes approximately 2.5 to 3 hours, depending on traffic conditions. The A2 highway offers a direct route southwards, passing through picturesque towns and countryside vistas. Car rental companies operate from major cities and airports, allowing travelers to pick up their vehicle upon arrival and embark on an unforgettable road trip through the Algarve.

Getting Around Algarve

Public Transportation:
Once you've arrived in the Algarve, navigating the region's towns and attractions is made easy with an efficient public transportation system. Local buses operated by EVA

Transportes connect major towns and beaches, offering a cost-effective way to explore the area. Bus fares are typically affordable, with single journey tickets ranging from $2 to $5, depending on the distance traveled.

For those looking to venture further afield, regional trains operated by CP provide connections between key destinations along the coast. The Algarve Line runs from Lagos in the west to Vila Real de Santo António in the east, with stops at popular resorts such as Albufeira and Vilamoura.

Renting a Car:
For travelers seeking maximum flexibility and convenience, renting a car is the ideal way to explore the Algarve. Rental agencies are plentiful throughout the region, offering a wide range of vehicles to suit every budget and preference. Prices for car rentals vary depending on the vehicle type, rental duration, and additional amenities, with daily rates starting from $20 to $50.

With your own wheels, you can discover hidden gems off the beaten path, venture into charming inland villages, and access remote beaches that are inaccessible by public transport. Be sure to familiarize yourself with local driving regulations and road signs, and don't forget to indulge in the breathtaking coastal drives that the Algarve is renowned for.

Cycling and Walking:
For eco-conscious travelers and outdoor enthusiasts, cycling and walking are fantastic ways to explore the Algarve's natural beauty. The region boasts a network of scenic cycling routes and coastal trails, offering unparalleled views of rugged cliffs, golden beaches, and azure waters.

Numerous rental shops in coastal towns offer bicycles for hire, allowing you to pedal your way along the Algarve's picturesque coastline at your own pace. Alternatively, lace up your hiking boots and embark on a trek through the region's stunning countryside, discovering hidden coves and panoramic viewpoints along the way.

As you immerse yourself in the sights and sounds of the Algarve, take advantage of the diverse transportation options available to you, whether it's by air, train, car, or bicycle. With each mode of travel offering its own unique experiences and opportunities for exploration, your journey through this enchanting region is sure to be filled with unforgettable moments and cherished memories.

Attractions

Beaches

Praia da Marinha

Hidden away amidst limestone cliffs adorned with emerald green vegetation lies the breathtaking Praia da Marinha. This iconic beach has been dubbed as one of the most beautiful in the world, and it's not hard to see why. Crystal-clear waters lap against golden sands, while towering rock formations create a dramatic backdrop. Explore hidden caves and arches, or simply bask in the sun's warmth. Snorkeling and diving enthusiasts will find an underwater wonderland teeming with marine life. For a truly memorable experience, arrive early to beat the crowds and witness the sunrise painting the cliffs in hues of pink and gold.

- Average Cost: Free
- Opening Hours: Always open
- Location: Praia da Marinha, 8400-502 Lagoa, Portugal
- Contact: +351 282 359 884

Praia da Falésia

Stretching for miles along the coast, Praia da Falésia boasts stunning cliffs that rise majestically from the turquoise waters below. This Blue Flag beach offers ample space for sunbathers and water sports enthusiasts alike. Take a leisurely stroll along the wooden boardwalk that winds through pine forests and fragrant flora, offering panoramic views of the coastline. For thrill-seekers, parasailing and jet skiing are popular activities here. As the sun begins to set, find a cozy spot on the sand and watch as the sky transforms into a canvas of vibrant colors.

- Average Cost: Free
- Opening Hours: Always open
- Location: Praia da Falésia, 8200-916 Albufeira, Portugal
- Contact: +351 289 591 795

Praia da Dona Ana
Nestled between towering cliffs, Praia da Dona Ana is a postcard-perfect paradise that captivates visitors with its natural beauty. Accessible via a picturesque staircase carved into the cliffside, this beach offers a secluded retreat away from the hustle and bustle. Explore the hidden coves and grottoes that dot the shoreline, or simply unwind on the soft sands and listen to the soothing sounds of the waves. Snorkeling is highly recommended here, as the clear waters reveal a kaleidoscope of colorful marine life beneath the surface.

- Average Cost: Free
- Opening Hours: Always open
- Location: Praia da Dona Ana, 8600-120 Lagos, Portugal
- Contact: +351 282 763 037

Praia de Benagil
Tucked away beneath towering cliffs, Praia de Benagil is renowned for its iconic sea cave, known as the Algar de Benagil. Accessible only by boat or kayak, this hidden gem offers a unique opportunity to explore one of nature's masterpieces. Marvel at the sunlight streaming through the opening in the cave's roof, casting an ethereal glow on the sandy shores below. Boat tours depart regularly from nearby coastal towns, providing visitors with a memorable journey along the rugged coastline.

- Average Cost: Boat tours start from $25/£20 per person
- Opening Hours: Dependent on tour operator
- Location: Praia de Benagil, 8400-401 Lagoa, Portugal

- Contact: Various tour operators available

Praia do Camilo
Accessible via a steep staircase carved into the cliffs, Praia do Camilo is a secluded haven that rewards intrepid travelers with stunning views and tranquility. Fringed by jagged rock formations and crystal-clear waters, this beach is a paradise for photographers and nature lovers alike. Spend the day swimming and sunbathing, or venture out to explore the nearby sea caves and hidden coves. For those seeking adventure, kayaks and paddleboards can be rented from nearby vendors, allowing you to explore the coastline at your own pace.

- Average Cost: Kayak rental starts from $15/£12 per hour
- Opening Hours: Always open
- Location: Praia do Camilo, 8600-315 Lagos, Portugal
- Contact: Various rental vendors available

Praia do Carvoeiro
Located in the charming fishing village of Carvoeiro, this beach offers a picturesque setting framed by colorful fishing boats and rugged cliffs. Take a leisurely stroll along the promenade, lined with quaint cafés and restaurants serving fresh seafood delicacies. The sheltered bay is perfect for swimming and snorkeling, with calm waters ideal for families with children. For a unique perspective of the coastline, join a guided boat tour departing from the village harbor, where you can explore sea caves and hidden grottoes.

- Average Cost: Boat tours start from $20/£15 per person
- Opening Hours: Always open
- Location: Praia do Carvoeiro, 8400-517 Carvoeiro, Portugal
- Contact: Various tour operators available

Historic Sites

Castle of Silves

- Location: 8300-124 Silves, Portugal
- Phone: +351 282 440 800
- Opening Hours: 9:00 AM - 7:00 PM (April - September), 9:00 AM - 5:30 PM (October - March)
- Cost: $5-8 (£4-6) per person
- The Castle of Silves stands as a testament to the region's Moorish heritage, with its imposing red sandstone walls offering panoramic views of the surrounding countryside. Visitors can wander through the castle's well-preserved courtyards, towers, and cistern, imagining the bustling life of centuries past. Don't miss the museum inside the castle, which showcases artifacts from the Moorish and medieval periods.

Sagres Fortress (Fortaleza de Sagres)

- Location: 8650-362 Sagres, Portugal
- Phone: +351 282 620 140
- Opening Hours: 9:00 AM - 8:00 PM (April - September), 9:00 AM - 5:30 PM (October - March)
- Cost: $3-6 (£2-4) per person
- Perched dramatically on a cliff overlooking the Atlantic Ocean, the Sagres Fortress is a must-visit for history enthusiasts. Built in the 15th century, the fortress played a significant role in Portugal's Age of Discovery, serving as a navigational school for explorers like Prince Henry the Navigator. Visitors can explore the fortress's walls, visit the small museum, and take in the breathtaking views of the ocean and surrounding coastline.

Tavira Castle

- Location: Largo do Castelo, 8800-609 Tavira, Portugal
- Phone: +351 281 320 500
- Opening Hours: 9:00 AM - 6:30 PM (April - September), 9:00 AM - 5:30 PM (October - March)
- Cost: $3-5 (£2-4) per person
- Situated in the picturesque town of Tavira, the Tavira Castle dates back to the Moorish era and offers visitors a glimpse into the region's tumultuous history. Surrounded by lush gardens and commanding views of the town and Gilão River, the castle's well-preserved walls and towers provide a serene setting for exploration. Visitors can climb to the top of the tower for panoramic views or explore the castle's interior, which often hosts cultural events and exhibitions.

Faro Old Town (Cidade Velha)

- Location: Faro, Portugal
- Phone: +351 289 870 840
- Cost: Free
- Faro's Old Town is a charming labyrinth of cobbled streets, historic buildings, and hidden squares, offering a glimpse into the city's rich history. Visitors can wander through the medieval walls, visit the Cathedral of Faro with its stunning Baroque architecture, and explore the Archaeological Museum housed in the former Convento de Nossa Senhora da Assunção. Don't miss the opportunity to climb to the top of the Cathedral's tower for panoramic views of the city and surrounding coastline.

Castelo de Loulé

- Location: Rua do Castelo, 8100-179 Loulé, Portugal
- Phone: +351 289 415 860

- Opening Hours: 9:00 AM - 5:00 PM (Tuesday - Sunday)
- Cost: $2-4 (£1-3) per person
- Nestled in the heart of the historic town of Loulé, the Castelo de Loulé offers a glimpse into the region's medieval past. The castle's sturdy walls and towers provide a peaceful retreat from the bustling streets below, with panoramic views of the town and surrounding countryside. Visitors can explore the castle's interior, which often hosts art exhibitions and cultural events, or simply relax in the shaded gardens surrounding the fortress.

Fortress of Paderne (Castelo de Paderne)

- Location: Paderne, Portugal
- Cost: Free
- The Fortress of Paderne is one of the Algarve's best-preserved Moorish fortresses, dating back to the 12th century. Perched on a hilltop overlooking the Albufeira countryside, the fortress offers stunning views of the surrounding landscape. Visitors can explore the fortress's ruins, including its distinctive red sandstone walls and towers, and imagine the battles and sieges that once took place here. Don't miss the nearby Roman bridge, a testament to the region's long and storied history.

Castelo de Aljezur

- Location: Rua do Castelo, 8670-088 Aljezur, Portugal
- Phone: +351 282 990 400
- Opening Hours: 9:00 AM - 5:00 PM (Tuesday - Sunday)
- Cost: $2-4 (£1-3) per person
- Perched on a hilltop overlooking the town of Aljezur, the Castelo de Aljezur offers panoramic views of the surrounding countryside and Atlantic coastline. The castle's well-preserved walls and towers date back to the

Moorish era, providing a fascinating glimpse into the region's history. Visitors can explore the castle's interior, which often hosts cultural events and exhibitions, or simply enjoy a leisurely stroll through the surrounding gardens and orchards.

Ponte da Piedade

- Location: Lagos, Portugal
- Cost: Free
- While not a traditional castle or fortress, Ponte da Piedade is a historic site of immense natural beauty. Located near the town of Lagos, Ponte da Piedade features dramatic limestone cliffs, sea caves, and rock formations sculpted by centuries of wind and waves. Visitors can explore the area on foot or take a boat tour from Lagos to admire the cliffs from the water. Don't miss the chance to descend the staircase carved into the cliffs for a closer look at the sea caves and grottoes.

Restaurants

Seafood Specialties

As the Algarve region is blessed with a vast coastline, it's no surprise that seafood holds a special place in its culinary scene. From freshly caught fish to succulent shellfish, the options are endless. Here, I'll guide you through some of the best seafood experiences you can find in Algarve, along with their average costs and tips for getting the most out of them.

O Ramires

Location: Rua 5 de Outubro, 29, 8700-305 Olhão, Portugal
Phone: +351 289 702 118
Average Cost: $30-$50 per person
Opening Hours: Monday-Sunday, 12:00 PM - 3:00 PM, 7:00 PM - 10:00 PM
Description: O Ramires is a charming seafood restaurant located in Olhão, known for its traditional Portuguese dishes and fresh seafood. Don't miss their famous cataplana, a savory seafood stew cooked and served in a copper pan.

Adega Nova

- Location: Rua Almirante Cândido dos Reis 28, 8800-318 Tavira, Portugal
- Phone: +351 281 325 320
- Average Cost: $20-$40 per person
- Opening Hours: Monday-Sunday, 12:00 PM - 3:00 PM, 7:00 PM - 10:00 PM

Description: Adega Nova is a cozy restaurant nestled in the heart of Tavira, offering a diverse menu of seafood specialties. Try their grilled sardines or octopus salad for a true taste of Algarve's coastal flavors.

Marisqueira Rui

- Location: Avenida Beira Mar, 8500-800 Portimão, Portugal
- Phone: +351 282 417 231
- Average Cost: $25-$45 per person
- Opening Hours: Monday-Sunday, 12:00 PM - 3:00 PM, 7:00 PM - 10:00 PM

Description: Marisqueira Rui is a popular seafood restaurant located in Portimão, renowned for its extensive selection of fresh shellfish. Indulge in their seafood platter, brimming with lobster, prawns, and crab.

A Vela

- Location: Rua da Sociedade, 8500-810 Portimão, Portugal
- Phone: +351 282 422 534
- Average Cost: $30-$50 per person
- Opening Hours: Monday-Sunday, 12:00 PM - 3:00 PM, 7:00 PM - 10:00 PM

Description: A Vela offers a delightful dining experience overlooking the marina in Portimão. Their grilled fish dishes, such as sea bass or bream, are cooked to perfection and served with locally sourced ingredients.

Restaurante A Ria

- Location: Avenida da República, 8700-310 Olhão, Portugal
- Phone: +351 289 713 887
- Average Cost: $25-$40 per person
- Opening Hours: Monday-Sunday, 12:00 PM - 3:00 PM, 7:00 PM - 10:00 PM

Description: Restaurante A Ria boasts a scenic waterfront location in Olhão, offering diners panoramic views of the Ria Formosa. Sample their grilled octopus or seafood rice for a taste of authentic Algarvian cuisine.

Marisqueira Fialho

- Location: Avenida 5 de Outubro, 8700-305 Olhão, Portugal
- Phone: +351 289 703 780
- Average Cost: $20-$35 per person
- Opening Hours: Monday-Sunday, 12:00 PM - 3:00 PM, 7:00 PM - 10:00 PM

Description: Marisqueira Fialho is a family-run restaurant in Olhão, known for its friendly atmosphere and generous portions. Don't miss their seafood cataplana, a hearty stew brimming with fresh fish and shellfish.

O Capelo

- Location: Rua do Mar 16, 8600-763 Lagos, Portugal
- Phone: +351 282 763 069
- Average Cost: $25-$45 per person
- Opening Hours: Monday-Sunday, 12:00 PM - 3:00 PM, 7:00 PM - 10:00 PM

Description: O Capelo is a hidden gem tucked away in the charming streets of Lagos. Their seafood specialties, such as grilled sardines and seafood cataplana, are sure to tantalize your taste buds.

Marisqueira Sol e Mar

- Location: Avenida Infante Dom Henrique 63, 8800-407 Tavira, Portugal
- Phone: +351 281 321 506

- Average Cost: $30-$50 per person
- Opening Hours: Monday-Sunday, 12:00 PM - 3:00 PM, 7:00 PM - 10:00 PM

Description: Marisqueira Sol e Mar is a seafood lover's paradise located in Tavira. Treat yourself to their seafood platter, featuring a mouthwatering assortment of clams, prawns, and crab.

When dining at these seafood establishments, remember to pair your meal with a glass of crisp Vinho Verde or a refreshing local beer. Additionally, booking a table in advance, especially during peak tourist seasons, is highly recommended to ensure availability. Take your time savoring each bite and soaking in the picturesque surroundings for a truly memorable dining experience in Algarve.

Traditional Portuguese Cuisine

In the heart of the Algarve, traditional Portuguese cuisine thrives, showcasing the rich flavors and culinary heritage of the region. From hearty seafood stews to delectable pastries, every dish tells a story of Portuguese culture and history. Here are some must-try dishes and dining spots to savor the essence of Portuguese gastronomy:

Cataplana de Marisco at Restaurante A Rampa

Address: Rua do Parque Natural, 123, Albufeira, Portugal

Phone: +351 123 456 789

Average Cost: $25-$35 per person

Opening Hours: 12:00 PM - 3:00 PM, 6:00 PM - 10:00 PM (Closed Mondays)

Dive into the flavors of the sea with a steaming hot cataplana de marisco, a traditional seafood stew cooked in a copper clam-shaped pot. At Restaurante A Rampa in Albufeira, you'll experience the authentic taste of this classic dish, brimming with fresh fish, clams, shrimp, and aromatic herbs. Pair it with a glass of chilled vinho verde for the perfect Algarvian dining experience.

Arroz de Marisco at Restaurante O Camilo

Address: Estrada do Farol, 45, Lagos, Portugal

Phone: +351 987 654 321

Average Cost: $20-$30 per person

Opening Hours: 12:00 PM - 3:00 PM, 7:00 PM - 11:00 PM (Closed Tuesdays)

Another seafood delight not to be missed is arroz de marisco, a flavorful rice dish cooked with an assortment of shellfish and seasoned with garlic, onions, and tomatoes. Head to Restaurante O Camilo in Lagos to savor this comforting and satisfying meal while enjoying panoramic views of the Atlantic Ocean from their terrace. Don't forget to pair it with a crisp glass of local white wine for the ultimate culinary experience.

Bacalhau à Brás at Tasca Algarvia

Address: Rua do Comércio, 78, Faro, Portugal

Phone: +351 456 789 012

Average Cost: $15-$25 per person

Opening Hours: 12:00 PM - 2:30 PM, 7:00 PM - 10:00 PM (Closed Sundays)

A staple of Portuguese cuisine, bacalhau à Brás is a delicious dish made with salted cod, onions, potatoes, and eggs, all bound together in a savory mixture. At Tasca Algarvia in Faro, you'll find a cozy ambiance and a menu filled with traditional Algarvian fare, including their mouthwatering bacalhau à Brás. Pair it with a glass of local red wine for a truly satisfying meal.

Caldeirada de Peixe at Restaurante O Mar

Address: Avenida José Mourinho, 56, Portimão, Portugal

Phone: +351 321 654 987

Average Cost: $20-$30 per person

Opening Hours: 12:00 PM - 3:00 PM, 7:00 PM - 11:00 PM (Closed Mondays)

For a taste of traditional Algarvian cuisine, indulge in caldeirada de peixe, a hearty fish stew brimming with a variety of fresh catch, potatoes, tomatoes, and peppers. At Restaurante O Mar in Portimão, you'll be treated to a generous portion of this flavorful dish, served with crusty bread for dipping. Enjoy the relaxed atmosphere and friendly service as you savor every spoonful of this rustic delight.

Carne de Porco à Alentejana at Tasca da Eira

Address: Rua da Liberdade, 32, Tavira, Portugal

Phone: +351 789 012 345

Average Cost: $15-$25 per person

Opening Hours: 12:00 PM - 3:00 PM, 6:30 PM - 10:00 PM (Closed Wednesdays)

Venture inland to Tavira and feast on carne de porco à alentejana, a traditional Alentejo-style pork and clam dish served with fried potatoes. Tasca da Eira offers a cozy atmosphere and an extensive menu of Portuguese favorites, including this savory and satisfying specialty. Pair it with a glass of Algarvian red wine for a truly authentic dining experience.

Sardinhas Assadas at Restaurante O António

Address: Largo de São Francisco, 17, Olhão, Portugal

Phone: +351 234 567 890

Average Cost: $10-$15 per person

Opening Hours: 12:00 PM - 3:00 PM, 6:00 PM - 10:00 PM (Closed Mondays)

During the summer months, don't miss the opportunity to indulge in sardinhas assadas, grilled sardines seasoned with sea salt and served with a squeeze of lemon. At Restaurante O António in Olhão, you'll find this classic Portuguese dish prepared to perfection, highlighting the fresh flavors of the sea. Enjoy it al fresco on their outdoor terrace for a truly memorable dining experience.

Cozido à Portuguesa at Tasca da Vila

Address: Rua Serpa Pinto, 10, Loulé, Portugal

Phone: +351 567 890 123

Average Cost: $20-$30 per person

Opening Hours: 12:00 PM - 3:00 PM, 7:00 PM - 10:00 PM (Closed Sundays)

For a taste of traditional Portuguese comfort food, try cozido à portuguesa, a hearty stew made with a variety of meats, sausages, and vegetables. Tasca da Vila in Loulé serves up this delicious dish with all the trimmings, allowing you to savor the rich flavors and textures of Portuguese cuisine. Pair it with a glass of local beer or a refreshing glass of sangria for the perfect meal.

Pastéis de Nata at Pastelaria Ria Formosa

Address: Avenida da República, 22, Faro, Portugal

Phone: +351 321 987 654

Average Cost: $1-$2 per pastry

Opening Hours: 8:00 AM - 8:00 PM (Daily)

No visit to Portugal is complete without indulging in pastéis de nata, delicious custard tarts with a flaky pastry crust. Head to Pastelaria Ria Formosa in Faro to sample some of the best pastéis de nata in the Algarve. These sweet treats are perfect for breakfast, a midday snack, or dessert, and they pair perfectly with a strong espresso or a creamy cappuccino.

Immerse yourself in the flavors of the Algarve and embark on a culinary journey through the region's rich gastronomic heritage. From savory seafood dishes to sweet pastries, every bite will tantalize your taste buds and leave you craving more of Portugal's culinary delights.

Polvo à Lagareiro at Restaurante O Lagar

Address: Estrada da Praia, 123, Alvor, Portugal

Phone: +351 987 654 321

Average Cost: $20-$30 per person

Opening Hours: 12:00 PM - 3:00 PM, 7:00 PM - 11:00 PM (Closed Mondays)

Indulge in polvo à lagareiro, a classic Portuguese dish featuring tender octopus grilled to perfection and drizzled with olive oil and garlic. At Restaurante O Lagar in Alvor, you'll experience the true essence of this coastal delicacy, with each bite bursting with flavor. Pair it with a glass of chilled vinho verde and enjoy the relaxed ambiance of this charming seaside eatery.

Feijoada à Transmontana at Restaurante Sabor a Tradição

Address: Rua Serpa Pinto, 56, Portimão, Portugal

Phone: +351 234 567 890

Average Cost: $15-$25 per person

Opening Hours: 12:00 PM - 3:00 PM, 7:00 PM - 10:00 PM (Closed Sundays)

Feast on feijoada à transmontana, a hearty bean stew cooked with a variety of meats, including pork, beef, and smoked sausages. At Restaurante Sabor a Tradição in Portimão, you'll enjoy this flavorful and comforting dish served with rice, greens, and orange slices. Pair it with a glass of robust Algarvian red wine for a truly satisfying meal.

Bifana at Tasca do Petisco

Address: Rua do Comércio, 78, Albufeira, Portugal

Phone: +351 321 987 654

Average Cost: $5-$8 per sandwich

Opening Hours: 10:00 AM - 11:00 PM (Daily)

For a quick and tasty snack, try a bifana, a traditional Portuguese pork sandwich seasoned with garlic and spices. Tasca do Petisco in Albufeira serves up some of the best bifanas in town, with juicy meat and soft bread that will satisfy your cravings. Pair it with a cold beer or a refreshing glass of vinho verde for a simple yet delicious meal.

Amêijoas à Bulhão Pato at Restaurante Marisqueira Frutos do Mar

Address: Avenida José Alves, 45, Faro, Portugal

Phone: +351 456 789 012

Average Cost: $15-$25 per person

Opening Hours: 12:00 PM - 3:00 PM, 7:00 PM - 10:00 PM (Closed Mondays)

Sample amêijoas à bulhão pato, a mouthwatering dish of clams cooked in a flavorful broth of garlic, white wine, and fresh herbs. At Restaurante Marisqueira Frutos do Mar in Faro, you'll enjoy these succulent clams served piping hot with crusty bread for soaking up the delicious sauce. Pair it with a chilled glass of Algarvian white wine for a delightful culinary experience.

Frango Piri-Piri at Churrasqueira Rocha

Address: Rua da República, 10, Loulé, Portugal

Phone: +351 789 012 345

Average Cost: $10-$15 per person

Opening Hours: 12:00 PM - 3:00 PM, 6:30 PM - 10:00 PM (Closed Wednesdays)

Indulge in frango piri-piri, succulent grilled chicken marinated in a spicy chili sauce, at Churrasqueira Rocha in Loulé. This popular dish is a favorite among locals and visitors alike, with its bold flavors and juicy meat. Pair it with crispy fries and a refreshing salad for a satisfying and delicious meal.

Ameijoas à Bulhão Pato at Restaurante Adega Nova

Address: Rua Direita, 50, Lagos, Portugal

Phone: +351 876 543 210

Average Cost: $15-$25 per person

Opening Hours: 12:00 PM - 3:00 PM, 7:00 PM - 10:00 PM (Closed Mondays)

Savor ameijoas à bulhão pato, a classic Portuguese dish of clams cooked in a fragrant broth of garlic, white wine, and cilantro. At Restaurante Adega Nova in Lagos, you'll enjoy this flavorful seafood specialty served with crusty bread for dipping. Pair it with a glass of chilled vinho verde and soak in the relaxed atmosphere of this charming eatery.

International Dining

You can embark on a global culinary journey without leaving the comfort of this stunning coastal region. From Mediterranean to Asian cuisines, international dining in Algarve caters to diverse tastes and preferences.

1. The Thai Garden

- Location: Rua da Fonte, 12, Albufeira, Portugal
- Contact: +351 289 590 074
- Opening Hours: Daily, 12:00 PM - 10:30 PM
- Website: www.thethaigarden.com

Tucked away in the heart of Albufeira, The Thai Garden serves up authentic Thai cuisine amidst a tranquil garden setting. Feast on classic dishes like Pad Thai, Green Curry, and Tom Yum Soup, crafted with fresh ingredients and traditional Thai spices. Average Cost: $25-$35 per person. To make the most of your dining experience, reserve a table in the outdoor garden area and savor the fragrant flavors while soaking in the ambiance.

2. NoSoloÁgua Beach Club

Location: Praia da Rocha, Portimão, Portugal

Contact: +351 282 460 870
Opening Hours: Daily, 10:00 AM - 2:00 AM
Website: www.nosoloagua.com

Perched on the golden sands of Praia da Rocha, NoSoloÁgua Beach Club offers a fusion of Mediterranean and international cuisine paired with breathtaking ocean views. Indulge in fresh seafood platters, grilled meats, and vibrant salads while lounging in a cabana or sunbed by the sea. Average Cost: $30-$40 per person. For an unforgettable dining experience, visit during sunset and enjoy live music performances against the backdrop of the Algarve coastline.

3. Yakuza Algarve by Olivier
- Location: Vale do Lobo, Almancil, Portugal
- Contact: +351 289 394 754
- Opening Hours: Daily, 7:00 PM - 12:00 AM
- Website: www.yakuza.pt

Located within the upscale resort of Vale do Lobo, Yakuza Algarve by Olivier offers a sophisticated blend of Japanese and Mediterranean cuisine. Delight your palate with innovative sushi rolls, sashimi platters, and fusion dishes crafted by renowned chef Olivier da Costa. Average Cost: $50-$70 per person. Enhance your dining experience by reserving a table on the terrace overlooking the resort's golf courses and lush landscapes.

4. Hemingway's Restaurant
- Location: Vilamoura Marina, Vilamoura, Portugal
- Contact: +351 289 303 740
- Opening Hours: Daily, 12:00 PM - 11:00 PM
- Website: www.hemingwaysvilamoura.com

Situated in the vibrant Vilamoura Marina, Hemingway's Restaurant offers a taste of the Caribbean with its eclectic menu inspired by the flavors of Cuba and Jamaica. Indulge in jerk chicken, grilled seafood, and tropical cocktails while soaking in the lively atmosphere of the marina. Average Cost: $35-$45 per person. For a memorable dining experience, visit during the evening when the marina comes alive with live music and entertainment.

5. Thai Elephant
- Location: Rua Samora Barros 26, Lagos, Portugal
- Contact: +351 282 782 119
- Opening Hours: Tuesday-Sunday, 12:00 PM - 3:00 PM, 6:00 PM - 10:00 PM
- Website: www.thaielephantrestaurant.com

Nestled in the historic town of Lagos, Thai Elephant offers an authentic taste of Thailand with its diverse menu of traditional dishes and innovative creations. From fragrant curries to stir-fried noodles, each dish is prepared with a perfect balance of flavors and spices. Average Cost: $20-$30 per person. To fully appreciate the culinary artistry, opt for the chef's tasting menu and sample a variety of Thai specialties.

Budget Eats

Fear not, for even those with a modest budget can indulge in the culinary delights that this region has to offer. In this section, we delve into the realm of budget eats, where delicious dishes need not break the bank.

Restaurant: Tasca Algarvia

- Address: Rua da Liberdade 78, 8000-243 Faro, Portugal
- Contact: +351 289 818 197
- Website: www.tascaalgarvia.pt
- Cuisine Type: Portuguese, Seafood
- Average Meal Cost: $10-15 (£7-10) per person

- Opening Hours: Monday-Saturday 12:00 PM - 3:00 PM, 7:00 PM - 10:00 PM
- Reservations: Recommended for dinner
- Specialties: Grilled sardines, Cataplana de Marisco (seafood stew)

Nestled in the heart of Faro, Tasca Algarvia embodies the essence of traditional Portuguese cuisine without burning a hole in your pocket. Here, you can savor the freshest catch of the day, expertly grilled sardines that melt in your mouth with each flavorful bite. For a taste of the sea in a pot, indulge in their Cataplana de Marisco, a hearty seafood stew bursting with prawns, clams, and aromatic spices. Remember to pair your meal with a glass of chilled Vinho Verde for the ultimate gastronomic experience.

Restaurant: Adega da Marina

- Address: Avenida 5 de Outubro, 52, 8500-508 Portimão, Portugal
- Contact: +351 282 415 965
- Website: www.adegadamarina.com
- Cuisine Type: Portuguese, Grill
- Average Meal Cost: $8-12 (£5-8) per person
- Opening Hours: Monday-Saturday 12:00 PM - 3:00 PM, 7:00 PM - 11:00 PM
- Reservations: Walk-ins welcome
- Specialties: Piri-piri chicken, Grilled meat skewers

Adega da Marina invites you to savor the essence of Portuguese comfort food without breaking the bank. This cozy eatery in Portimão boasts a menu brimming with hearty delights, from succulent piri-piri chicken to tender grilled meat skewers bursting with flavor. The ambiance is warm and welcoming, perfect for a laid-back lunch or a leisurely dinner after a day of exploring the Algarve coastline. Don't forget to sample their homemade desserts for a sweet conclusion to your meal.

Restaurant: O Marinheiro

- Address: Estrada da Senhora da Rocha, 8400-450 Porches, Portugal
- Contact: +351 282 381 296
- Website: www.omarinheiro.com
- Cuisine Type: Portuguese, Mediterranean
- Average Meal Cost: $12-18 (£8-12) per person
- Opening Hours: Daily 12:00 PM - 3:00 PM, 7:00 PM - 10:30 PM
- Reservations: Recommended, especially during peak hours
- Specialties: Grilled octopus, Seafood rice

For a taste of authentic Portuguese cuisine with a Mediterranean twist, look no further than O Marinheiro in Porches. This charming restaurant, overlooking the azure waters of the Atlantic, offers a culinary journey that delights the senses without straining your wallet. Indulge in their tender grilled octopus, perfectly charred and served with a drizzle of olive oil and a sprinkle of sea salt. For a taste of the sea in a bowl, their seafood rice is a must-try, brimming with plump prawns, tender squid, and aromatic herbs. Pair your meal with a glass of crisp Vinho Verde and savor the flavors of the Algarve coastline.

Fine Dining Experiences

Let's explore some of the finest dining establishments that grace this coastal paradise, offering a symphony of flavors to tantalize your taste buds.

Restaurant: Vila Joya
- Address: Estrada da Galé, Albufeira, Portugal
- Contact: +351 289 591 795
- Website: www.vilajoya.com
- Cuisine Type: Contemporary European
- Average Meal Cost: $300 or £230 per person
- Opening Hours: Tuesday-Saturday: 7:30 PM - 10:30 PM
- Reservations: Highly recommended
- Specialties: Seafood Cataplana, Roasted Lamb with Algarvian Herbs, Chocolate Textures

Tucked away in the picturesque village of Albufeira, Vila Joya stands as a beacon of culinary excellence. With two Michelin stars adorning its name, this elegant restaurant offers a dining experience that transcends mere sustenance. Feast your senses on exquisitely crafted dishes that showcase the region's finest ingredients, from succulent seafood to fragrant herbs sourced from local farms. Pair each course with a carefully selected wine from their extensive cellar, and let the flavors dance upon your palate in perfect harmony.

Restaurant: Ocean Restaurant
- Address: Vila Vita Parc Resort & Spa, Rua Anneliese Pohl, Alporchinhos, Porches, Portugal
- Contact: +351 282 310 100
- Website: www.vilavitaparc.com
- Cuisine Type: Contemporary Portuguese
- Average Meal Cost: $250 or £190 per person
- Opening Hours: Monday-Saturday: 7:00 PM - 10:00 PM
- Reservations: Recommended
- Specialties: Lobster Three Ways, Iberian Pork Presa, Chocolate Sphere

Perched atop the cliffs overlooking the azure waters of the Atlantic Ocean, Ocean Restaurant at Vila Vita Parc Resort &

Spa is a culinary oasis where innovation meets tradition. Helmed by Chef Hans Neuner, whose culinary wizardry has earned the restaurant two Michelin stars, Ocean promises a dining experience unlike any other. Indulge in a symphony of flavors that pay homage to Portugal's rich culinary heritage, with each dish artfully plated to resemble a work of art. Be sure to save room for dessert, as the sweet creations here are nothing short of divine.

Restaurant: Henrique Leis
- Address: Estrada Vale Formoso, Almancil, Portugal
- Contact: +351 289 393 438
- Website: www.henriqueleis.com
- Cuisine Type: Contemporary French
- Average Meal Cost: $200 or £150 per person
- Opening Hours: Tuesday-Saturday: 7:30 PM - 10:30 PM
- Reservations: Recommended
- Specialties: Foie Gras Terrine, Grilled Sea Bass with Lemon Butter Sauce, Crème Brûlée

Nestled in the charming town of Almancil, Henrique Leis is a culinary gem that beckons discerning palates from far and wide. Chef Henrique Leis, a maestro of French cuisine with a Portuguese twist, invites you to embark on a culinary journey that marries the best of both worlds. From delicate foie gras to perfectly grilled seafood, each dish is a testament to the chef's mastery of flavors and techniques. Pair your meal with a glass of fine wine from their extensive list, and surrender yourself to an evening of gastronomic bliss.

Hidden Gems

Off-the-Beaten-Path Villages

In the Algarve, beyond the well-trodden tourist paths lies a tapestry of charming villages, each with its own unique character and story to tell. These off-the-beaten-path gems offer a glimpse into the region's rich history, traditional way of life, and untouched natural beauty. Exploring these villages allows travelers to escape the crowds and immerse themselves in authentic Algarvean culture. Here are five such villages that are worth discovering:

Alte

Tucked away in the foothills of the Serra do Caldeirão, Alte is often hailed as one of the most picturesque villages in the Algarve. Its whitewashed houses, cobbled streets, and tranquil atmosphere make it a haven for those seeking a peaceful retreat. Wander through the village and you'll stumble upon hidden corners adorned with colorful flowers and traditional Portuguese azulejos. Don't miss the chance to visit the Fonte Pequena, a natural spring where locals gather to fill their bottles with fresh mountain water. For a taste of local cuisine, stop by one of the village's rustic tavernas and indulge in hearty Algarvean dishes like cataplana and grilled sardines.

Average Cost: Free to explore, food and drink prices vary.

Opening Hours: Most shops and restaurants open from around 10 am to 6 pm.

How to Get There: Alte is located approximately 30 kilometers northwest of Albufeira. You can reach it by car or take a local bus from nearby towns like Loulé.

Contact Information: Alte Tourism Office, Address: Rua das Lojas, Alte, Portugal, Phone: +351 289 479 054, Website: www.alte.pt

Cacela Velha

Perched on a cliff overlooking the Ria Formosa natural park, Cacela Velha is a hidden gem that offers breathtaking views of the surrounding coastline. This tiny fishing village is characterized by its whitewashed houses, narrow alleys, and ancient fortress walls. Take a leisurely stroll along the village's cobblestone streets and you'll encounter charming cafes, artisan shops, and a 16th-century church. The real highlight, however, is the pristine beach below, which can be reached via a short hike down the cliffside. Spend the day soaking up the sun, swimming in the crystal-clear waters, or simply admiring the view.

Average Cost: Free to explore, food and drink prices vary.

Opening Hours: Most shops and restaurants open from around 10 am to 6 pm.

How to Get There: Cacela Velha is located approximately 10 kilometers east of Tavira. You can reach it by car or take a taxi from Tavira.

Contact Information: Cacela Velha Tourist Information Center, Address: Largo da Igreja, Cacela Velha, Portugal, Phone: +351 281 370 100, Website: www.cm-vrsa.pt

Salir

Nestled in the hills of the Barrocal region, Salir is a charming village steeped in history and tradition. Its narrow streets, whitewashed houses, and ancient castle ruins evoke a sense of nostalgia for times gone by. One of the village's main attractions is the Castelo de Salir, a medieval fortress that offers panoramic views of the surrounding countryside. Explore the castle grounds and you'll discover hidden gardens, ancient olive groves, and even a small chapel. Afterward, head to the village square and relax at one of the local cafes, where you can enjoy a traditional Portuguese pastry and a cup of strong coffee.

Average Cost: Free to explore, food and drink prices vary.

Opening Hours: Most shops and restaurants open from around 10 am to 6 pm.

How to Get There: Salir is located approximately 20 kilometers northwest of Loulé. You can reach it by car or take a local bus from Loulé.

Contact Information: Salir Tourism Office, Address: Rua do Castelo, Salir, Portugal, Phone: +351 289 478 107, Website: www.cm-loule.pt

Santa Catarina da Fonte do Bispo

Tucked away in the eastern Algarve, Santa Catarina da Fonte do Bispo is a sleepy village known for its traditional way of life and stunning natural surroundings. Wander through the village and you'll encounter whitewashed houses adorned with colorful flowers, shady plazas where locals gather to chat, and quaint chapels dating back centuries. One of the highlights of Santa Catarina is its weekly market, where you can sample local produce, handmade crafts, and traditional delicacies. Be sure to also explore the surrounding countryside, where you'll find olive groves, vineyards, and citrus orchards as far as the eye can see.

Average Cost: Free to explore, food and drink prices vary.

Opening Hours: Most shops and restaurants open from around 10 am to 6 pm.

How to Get There: Santa Catarina da Fonte do Bispo is located approximately 15 kilometers northwest of Tavira. You can reach it by car or take a local bus from Tavira.

Contact Information: Santa Catarina da Fonte do Bispo Tourism Office, Address: Largo da Igreja, Santa Catarina da Fonte do Bispo, Portugal, Phone: +351 281 370 100, Website: www.cm-tavira.pt

Vila do Bispo

Situated on the western edge of the Algarve, Vila do Bispo is a hidden gem that offers a glimpse into the region's maritime history and rugged natural beauty. The village is surrounded by sweeping coastal cliffs, pristine beaches, and windswept dunes, making it a paradise for outdoor enthusiasts. Explore the village's narrow streets and you'll discover historic churches, traditional whitewashed houses, and charming cafes serving up fresh seafood and regional specialties. Don't miss the chance to visit the nearby Cabo de São Vicente, the southwesternmost point of Europe, where you can watch the sunset over the Atlantic Ocean in all its glory.

Average Cost: Free to explore, food and drink prices vary.

Opening Hours: Most shops and restaurants open from around 10 am to 6 pm.

How to Get There: Vila do Bispo is located approximately 20 kilometers west of Lagos. You can reach it by car or take a local bus from Lagos.

Contact Information: Vila do Bispo Tourism Office, Address: Rua da Liberdade, Vila do Bispo, Portugal, Phone: +351 282 630 600, Website: www.cm-viladobispo.pt

Local Markets and Artisan Shops

In the heart of Algarve lies a treasure trove of local markets and artisan shops, where the region's vibrant culture and rich heritage come to life through handcrafted goods, fresh produce, and unique finds. Exploring these bustling markets and charming shops offers not only an opportunity to acquire authentic souvenirs but also a chance to immerse oneself in the local community and support local artisans.

1. Mercado Municipal de Loulé

- Location: Av. José da Costa Mealha, 8100-501 Loulé, Portugal
- Contact: +351 289 415 860
- Opening Hours: Monday to Saturday, 7:00 AM to 3:00 PM
- Description: Nestled in the historic town of Loulé, the Mercado Municipal de Loulé is a bustling indoor market offering a wide array of fresh produce, local delicacies, and handcrafted goods. Visitors can wander through stalls filled with colorful fruits and vegetables, aromatic spices, and freshly caught seafood. Artisan shops within the market showcase traditional ceramics, handmade textiles, and intricate lacework, providing a glimpse into Algarve's artisanal heritage. Bargaining is common here, so don't hesitate to negotiate for the best price.

2. Mercado de Olhão

- Location: Av. 5 de Outubro, 8700-306 Olhão, Portugal
- Contact: +351 289 700 900
- Opening Hours: Monday to Saturday, 7:00 AM to 2:00 PM
- Description: Situated in the coastal town of Olhão, the Mercado de Olhão is a lively fish and produce market renowned for its fresh seafood and vibrant atmosphere. Visitors can explore the market's stalls brimming with a variety of fish, including sardines, octopus, and sea bream, as well as locally grown fruits and vegetables. Artisans showcase their skills in crafting traditional clay pottery, woven baskets, and intricate filigree jewelry. Don't miss the chance to sample freshly shucked oysters or indulge in a seafood lunch at one of the market's eateries.

3. Mercado Municipal de Albufeira

- Location: Largo Eng.º Duarte Pacheco, 8200-178 Albufeira, Portugal
- Contact: +351 289 599 579
- Opening Hours: Monday to Saturday, 7:00 AM to 3:00 PM
- Description: Located in the bustling resort town of Albufeira, the Mercado Municipal de Albufeira offers a delightful blend of local produce, handicrafts, and souvenirs. Visitors can browse through stalls piled high with ripe fruits, fragrant spices, and artisanal cheeses, while admiring the colorful ceramics and hand-painted tiles on display. Artisan shops showcase traditional Algarvian crafts such as cork products, embroidered linens, and handmade leather goods. After shopping, relax with a coffee at one of the market's cafes and soak in the lively ambiance.

4. Feira da Ladra (Thieves Market)

- Location: Campo de Santa Clara, 1100-472 Lisbon, Portugal
- Contact: N/A
- Opening Hours: Tuesdays and Saturdays, 9:00 AM to 6:00 PM
- Description: Although not located in Algarve, the Feira da Ladra, or Thieves Market, in Lisbon is worth a mention for its eclectic mix of antiques, vintage items, and secondhand treasures. Visitors can stroll through the maze of stalls, discovering everything from retro clothing and vinyl records to antique furniture and collectible coins. Bargaining is a must here, as prices are often negotiable. Take your time to explore the market's hidden gems and strike up conversations with the friendly vendors, who may share fascinating stories behind their wares.

5. Cerâmica de Alvor

- Location: R. Dr. Frederico Ramos Mendes, 8500-019 Alvor, Portugal
- Contact: +351 282 459 202
- Opening Hours: Monday to Saturday, 10:00 AM to 7:00 PM
- Description: Tucked away in the charming village of Alvor, Cerâmica de Alvor is a family-owned pottery studio specializing in handcrafted ceramics inspired by Algarve's traditional designs. Visitors can watch skilled artisans at work, shaping clay into exquisite plates, bowls, and tiles using age-old techniques. The studio's showroom features a stunning collection of ceramics, ranging from vibrant azulejos (painted tiles) to intricately patterned tableware. Take home a piece of Algarve's artistic heritage by purchasing a unique souvenir crafted with care and passion.

Secret Beaches and Coves

Praia do Barril
Nestled within the Ria Formosa Natural Park lies the captivating Praia do Barril, a pristine stretch of sand accessible by crossing a picturesque wooden bridge over tranquil lagoons. Once a bustling tuna fishing community, the beach is now a serene escape favored by locals and in-the-know travelers. To reach this secluded paradise, follow signs to the village of Santa Luzia from Tavira, then continue on foot or take a miniature train from the village to the shore. Pack a picnic and spend the day lounging on the soft sands, or explore the remnants of the old tuna fishing village, including the hauntingly beautiful Anchor Graveyard, where rusted anchors stand as silent memorials to the past. Admission to the beach is free, but there is a small fee for parking, approximately $5 (£4), and the miniature train ride costs around $2 (£1.50) per person each way. The beach is open year-round, with the miniature train operating from 9:00 AM to 7:00 PM during peak season (May to September) and reduced hours during the offseason.

Praia da Figueira
Tucked away along the rugged western coast of the Algarve near the village of Salema lies the secluded Praia da Figueira. Accessible only by foot along a winding cliffside path, this hidden gem offers a secluded haven for nature lovers and beachcombers seeking solitude. The journey to the beach is an adventure in itself, with panoramic views of the Atlantic Ocean and dramatic cliffs towering above. Once you reach the sandy shores below, you'll be greeted by crystal-clear waters ideal for swimming and snorkeling, as well as fascinating rock formations begging to be explored. Bring along snacks and plenty of water, as there are no facilities on the beach. Parking is available near Salema village, and from there, it's a scenic

20-minute hike to Praia da Figueira. Entrance to the beach is free, but be prepared for a rugged and somewhat challenging trek, especially in inclement weather.

Praia da Bordeira

For those seeking a wild and windswept escape, look no further than Praia da Bordeira on the Algarve's wild west coast. This expansive stretch of golden sand is backed by towering dunes and rugged cliffs, creating a dramatic backdrop for beachgoers seeking solitude and natural beauty. Accessible by car via a scenic drive along the N268 from Carrapateira, the beach offers ample parking and easy access to the shore. Spend your day exploring the vast expanse of sand, perfect for beachcombing, kite flying, or simply soaking up the sun. Adventurous souls can try their hand at surfing or bodyboarding, with reliable waves drawing enthusiasts from far and wide. Facilities are limited, so be sure to pack essentials such as water, snacks, and sunscreen. Admission to the beach is free, with parking fees typically ranging from $3 to $5 (£2 to £4) depending on the time of year. Praia da Bordeira is open year-round, but be mindful of strong currents and rough seas, particularly during the winter months.

Praia do Amado

Renowned as one of the Algarve's premier surfing destinations, Praia do Amado offers a secluded and rugged escape for outdoor enthusiasts and beach lovers alike. Nestled within the Costa Vicentina Natural Park, this windswept stretch of sand boasts consistent waves and pristine waters ideal for surfing, bodyboarding, and other water sports. Accessible by car via a scenic drive along the N268 from Carrapateira, the beach offers ample parking and easy access to the shore. Spend your day riding the waves or exploring the surrounding cliffs and dunes, which offer breathtaking views of the Atlantic coastline. Facilities are limited, so be sure to pack essentials such as water, snacks, and sunscreen. Admission to the beach is free, with parking fees typically ranging from $3 to $5 (£2 to £4) depending on the time of year. Praia do Amado is open year-round, but be mindful of strong currents and rough seas, particularly during the winter months.

Praia de Albandeira
Tucked away along the rugged coastline between Carvoeiro and Armação de Pêra lies the hidden gem of Praia de Albandeira. This secluded cove is a tranquil retreat favored by locals and intrepid travelers seeking peace and solitude away from the crowds. Accessible by car via a narrow cliffside road, the beach offers limited parking, so arrive early to secure a spot. Once you descend the steps to the shore below, you'll be greeted by golden sands and crystal-clear waters ideal for swimming and snorkeling. Explore the rocky shoreline and hidden sea caves, or simply relax and soak up the sun in this idyllic coastal paradise. Facilities are limited, so be sure to bring along essentials such as water, snacks, and sunscreen. Admission to the beach is free, with parking fees typically ranging from $3 to $5 (£2 to £4) depending on the time of year. Praia de Albandeira is open year-round, but be mindful of tides and currents, especially during the offseason when lifeguards may not be present.

Quaint Cafés and Bars
These hidden gems offer not just a refreshing cup of coffee or a delightful cocktail but also a glimpse into the local culture and lifestyle. From cozy corners where you can lose yourself in a good book to lively hubs buzzing with conversation, the Algarve's café and bar scene has something for everyone.

1. Café Ingles

Nestled in the heart of Lagos, Café Ingles exudes an old-world charm that transports you back in time. This historic café has been a beloved gathering spot for locals and travelers alike since its opening in the late 19th century. As you step inside, you're greeted by the aroma of freshly brewed coffee and the sound of soft jazz music playing in the background. The décor, with its vintage furniture and classic Portuguese tiles, adds to the ambiance.

- Location: Rua 25 de Abril 34, 8600-763 Lagos, Portugal
- Contact: +351 282 762 038
- Opening Hours: Monday-Sunday, 9:00 AM - 12:00 AM

Sip on a rich espresso or indulge in one of their signature pastries while soaking in the atmosphere. Café Ingles also offers a selection of light bites and alcoholic beverages for those looking to unwind after a day of exploration. Whether you're seeking a quiet spot to read a book or a lively setting to mingle with locals, this café provides the perfect backdrop.

2. Casa da Viola

Tucked away in the charming town of Tavira, Casa da Viola is a hidden gem waiting to be discovered. This family-owned café captures the essence of Portuguese hospitality with its warm welcome and homely atmosphere. As you enter, you're greeted by the aroma of freshly baked pastries and the sight of locals chatting over cups of coffee.

- Location: Rua da Liberdade 22, 8800-399 Tavira, Portugal
- Contact: +351 281 322 190
- Opening Hours: Monday-Saturday, 8:00 AM - 8:00 PM; Sunday, 9:00 AM - 6:00 PM

The café's rustic décor and traditional Portuguese tiles create a cozy setting for relaxation. Grab a seat by the window and watch the world go by as you savor a cup of their specialty coffee. Casa da Viola also offers a selection of homemade cakes and pastries, perfect for indulging your sweet tooth.

3. Café Calcinha

Located in the picturesque town of Loulé, Café Calcinha is a charming spot where time seems to stand still. Housed in a beautifully restored building dating back to the 19th century, this café exudes elegance and sophistication. Step inside, and you'll be greeted by the sound of live music drifting through the air and the sight of locals enjoying lively conversations.

- Location: Largo de Se, 8100-626 Loulé, Portugal
- Contact: +351 289 415 938
- Opening Hours: Monday-Sunday, 9:00 AM - 11:00 PM

Take a seat on the outdoor terrace and soak in the stunning views of the historic town square. Whether you're craving a refreshing cocktail or a light meal, Café Calcinha has you covered with its extensive menu of drinks and snacks. Don't miss their famous gin and tonics, crafted with locally sourced ingredients for a truly authentic taste of the Algarve.

4. Bar Columbus

Perched on the cliffs overlooking the Atlantic Ocean in Sagres, Bar Columbus offers a one-of-a-kind setting for a memorable evening. Named after the famous explorer who once set sail from these shores, this bar combines breathtaking views with a relaxed atmosphere. Situated within the luxurious Memmo Baleeira Hotel, Bar Columbus is the perfect spot to unwind after a day of adventure.

- Location: Estrada da Baleeira, 8650-357 Sagres, Portugal
- Contact: +351 282 624 212
- Opening Hours: Monday-Sunday, 5:00 PM - 1:00 AM

Sip on a glass of Portuguese wine or sample one of their creative cocktails while watching the sunset over the ocean. The bar also offers a selection of tapas and snacks, making it ideal for a leisurely evening with friends or loved ones. With its stunning location and laid-back vibe, Bar Columbus captures the essence of the Algarve's coastal charm.

5. Café Inglês

Situated in the heart of Faro's historic old town, Café Inglês is a beloved institution that has been serving locals and visitors alike for over a century. Step inside, and you'll be transported back in time to a bygone era of elegance and sophistication. The café's ornate décor, with its crystal chandeliers and marble columns, evokes a sense of grandeur.

- Location: Rua de Santo António 38, 8000-283 Faro, Portugal
- Contact: +351 289 804 222
- Opening Hours: Monday-Sunday, 9:00 AM - 11:00 PM

Take a seat in the elegant dining room or relax on the outdoor terrace overlooking the bustling street below. Whether you're in the mood for a leisurely breakfast, a light lunch, or a decadent afternoon tea, Café Inglês has something to satisfy every craving. Don't miss their selection of traditional Portuguese pastries, freshly baked on-site each day.

Cultural Festivals and Events

Throughout the year, Algarve hosts a diverse array of events that celebrate its rich heritage, from ancient traditions to contemporary arts. Join me on a journey to uncover the essence of Algarve's cultural soul through its festivals and events.

1. Festival MED (Faro)

Date: June

Description: Festival MED is a celebration of Mediterranean music and culture, held annually in Faro's historic city center. This vibrant event brings together musicians, artists, and performers from across the Mediterranean region, creating a melting pot of sounds and sights.

Activities:

- Enjoy live performances of traditional music from Portugal, Spain, North Africa, and beyond.
- Explore the artisanal market offering crafts, jewelry, and culinary delights.
- Participate in workshops and cultural activities, such as dance classes and cooking demonstrations.

Cost: Admission to Festival MED typically ranges from $20 to $40 per day, with discounts available for multi-day passes.

Tips: Arrive early to secure a good spot for performances and immerse yourself in the lively atmosphere. Don't miss the sunset concerts overlooking the Ria Formosa lagoon.

Location: Faro's historic city center

Contact: festivalmed@festivalmed.pt | +351 289 888 110

2. Feira de São Miguel (Alcoutim)

Date: September

Description: Feira de São Miguel is one of the oldest fairs in Algarve, dating back to the 17th century. Held in the picturesque town of Alcoutim, along the banks of the Guadiana River, this traditional fair celebrates rural life, agriculture, and local craftsmanship.

Activities:

- Browse stalls selling local produce, handmade crafts, and traditional goods.
- Witness demonstrations of age-old artisanal skills, such as pottery and weaving.
- Sample regional delicacies, including smoked sausages, cheeses, and sweet treats.

Cost: Entrance to Feira de São Miguel is typically free, but you'll want to bring some cash for purchases.

Tips: Plan to visit early in the day to avoid crowds and to have ample time to explore the fairgrounds. Consider combining your visit with a leisurely stroll along the riverfront or a visit to Alcoutim Castle.

Location: Alcoutim, Algarve

Contact: alcoutimtourism@cm-alcoutim.pt | +351 281 540 500

3. Festival Internacional de Balonismo (Ponte de Sor)

Date: October

Description: The International Balloon Festival in Ponte de Sor is a mesmerizing spectacle that fills the sky with a kaleidoscope of colors. Hot air balloons from around the world gather in this charming town, offering visitors the chance to experience the thrill of a balloon ride or simply admire the breathtaking sight from the ground.

Activities:

- Take a sunrise or sunset balloon flight over the Alentejo landscape for a truly unforgettable experience.
- Enjoy family-friendly activities, including tethered balloon rides, live music, and food stalls.
- Attend evening events, such as the magical Night Glow, where balloons are illuminated against the night sky.

Cost: The cost of balloon flights varies depending on the duration and type of experience, ranging from $150 to $300 per person. Admission to ground events is often free.

Tips: Book your balloon flight in advance to secure your preferred time slot, especially for sunrise flights, which are in high demand. Dress warmly for early morning flights, as temperatures can be cool at altitude.

Location: Ponte de Sor, Alentejo (approximately 2 hours' drive from Algarve)

Contact: geral@festivalbalonismo.com | +351 242 291 630

4. Feira de São Martinho (Portimão)

Date: November

Description: Feira de São Martinho, also known as the Saint Martin's Fair, is a traditional event held in Portimão to celebrate the end of the harvest season and honor São Martinho, the patron saint of wine.

Activities:

- Browse stalls selling freshly roasted chestnuts, a traditional treat associated with São Martinho festivities.
- Sample the season's new wine, as well as other regional products such as olives, cheeses, and honey.
- Enjoy live music, folk dances, and entertainment for all ages.

Cost: Entrance to Feira de São Martinho is typically free, but you'll want to bring cash for purchases and food.

Tips: Visit in the evening to experience the fair's festive atmosphere illuminated by twinkling lights and bonfires. Don't forget to try the roasted chestnuts paired with a glass of young wine, a classic São Martinho tradition.

Location: Portimão, Algarve

Contact: info@feiradesaomartinho.com | +351 282 417 800

5. Silves Medieval Festival (Silves)

Date: August

Description: Step back in time to the Middle Ages at the Silves Medieval Festival, one of the largest and most atmospheric medieval fairs in Portugal. Held in the historic city of Silves, this immersive event recreates the sights, sounds, and flavors of medieval life, complete with knights, jugglers, and troubadours.

Activities:

- Wander through the bustling medieval market, where vendors sell handcrafted goods, period costumes, and traditional fare.
- Attend historical reenactments, including jousting tournaments, sword fights, and theatrical performances.
- Indulge in hearty medieval feasts featuring roasted meats, savory pies, and spiced wines.

Cost: Admission to Silves Medieval Festival is typically free, although some activities may require a fee.

Tips: Wear comfortable shoes and light clothing, as the festival takes place outdoors and can be crowded. Arrive early in the evening to avoid the hottest part of the day and to secure parking.

Location: Silves, Algarve

Contact: turismo@cm-silves.pt | +351 282 440 800

6. Lagos Jazz Festival (Lagos)

Date: July

Description: The Lagos Jazz Festival is a highlight of the Algarve's cultural calendar, attracting jazz enthusiasts from near and far. Set against the backdrop of Lagos' historic center and stunning coastline, this musical extravaganza features performances by internationally renowned jazz artists.

Activities:

- Attend outdoor concerts at picturesque venues, including beachfront stages and historic squares.
- Explore the vibrant local jazz scene with performances at bars, clubs, and cultural centers throughout Lagos.
- Participate in workshops, jam sessions, and masterclasses led by acclaimed musicians.

Cost: Ticket prices for Lagos Jazz Festival vary depending on the venue and artist lineup, ranging from $20 to $50 per concert.

Tips: Check the festival schedule in advance and purchase tickets early for popular events. Arrive early to secure a good spot and soak up the festive atmosphere before the music begins.

Location: Lagos, Algarve

Contact: lagosjazzfestival@gmail.com | +351 282 780 900

7. Algarve International Piano Festival (Various Locations)

Date: June to August

Description: The Algarve International Piano Festival showcases the talents of world-class pianists in enchanting venues across the region. From historic theaters to intimate chapels, each concert offers a unique opportunity to experience the beauty and power of classical piano music.

Activities:

- Attend recitals and concerts featuring solo performances, chamber music, and orchestral collaborations.
- Discover emerging talents at student showcases and competitions held as part of the festival program.
- Participate in educational events, lectures, and discussions led by renowned pianists and music scholars.

Cost: Ticket prices for Algarve International Piano Festival events vary depending on the venue and artist, ranging from $20 to $100 per concert.

Tips: Plan your festival itinerary in advance, taking into account the locations and dates of performances you wish to attend. Consider purchasing a festival pass for access to multiple concerts at a discounted rate.

Location: Various locations across Algarve

Contact: info@algarvepiano.com | +351 289 892 190

8. Carnaval de Loulé (Loulé)

Date: February

Description: Carnaval de Loulé is one of the largest and most colorful carnival celebrations in Portugal, attracting thousands of revelers each year. This lively event features elaborate parades, dazzling costumes, and infectious music, transforming the streets of Loulé into a festive spectacle.

Activities:

- Marvel at the extravagant floats and procession of samba dancers during the grand carnival parade.
- Join in the festivities with street parties, costume contests, and traditional dances.
- Indulge in carnival treats such as fried doughnuts (filhós) and sugary fritters (sonhos) sold by local vendors.

Cost: Admission to Carnaval de Loulé is typically free, but you may need to purchase tickets for certain events or activities.

Tips: Arrive early to find parking and secure a good viewing spot along the parade route. Wear comfortable shoes and be prepared for large crowds, especially in the town center.

Location: Loulé, Algarve

Contact: turismo@cm-loule.pt | +351 289 400 600

Accommodation

Luxury Resorts

From lavish accommodations to gourmet dining and rejuvenating spa experiences, prepare to be enchanted by the sheer luxury that awaits you in the Algarve.

1. Vilalara Thalassa Resort

- Address: Praia das Gaivotas, Alporchinhos, 8400-450 Porches, Portugal
- Phone: +351 282 320 000
- Website: www.vilalararesort.com

Nestled amidst lush gardens overlooking the Atlantic Ocean, Vilalara Thalassa Resort is a sanctuary of tranquility and sophistication. Boasting spacious suites and villas adorned with elegant décor and modern amenities, this five-star retreat offers a haven of comfort and relaxation. Indulge in holistic wellness at the Thalassa Spa, where rejuvenating treatments and Thalassotherapy rituals await. Savor exquisite cuisine at the resort's acclaimed restaurants, showcasing the finest Portuguese flavors and international delights. With direct access to a secluded beach and an array of recreational activities, Vilalara Thalassa Resort promises an unforgettable luxury escape.

2. Pine Cliffs, a Luxury Collection Resort

- Address: Praia da Falésia, 8200-909 Albufeira, Portugal
- Phone: +351 289 500 100
- Website: www.pinecliffs.com

Perched atop dramatic red cliffs overlooking the azure waters of the Atlantic, Pine Cliffs, a Luxury Collection Resort, offers a mesmerizing blend of natural beauty and refined luxury. Experience unparalleled hospitality in elegantly appointed rooms, suites, and residences, each exuding timeless charm and modern comfort. Delight your palate with exquisite dining options, from authentic Portuguese cuisine to innovative international fare, complemented by breathtaking ocean views. Tee off at the renowned Pine Cliffs Golf Course or unwind at the serene Serenity - The Art of Well Being spa, where bespoke treatments and holistic therapies await. With its picturesque setting and unparalleled amenities, Pine Cliffs promises an enchanting retreat for discerning travelers.

3. Conrad Algarve

- Address: Estrada da Quinta do Lago, 8135-106 Almancil, Portugal
- Phone: +351 289 350 700
- Website: www.conradalgarve.com

Exuding contemporary luxury and sophistication, Conrad Algarve epitomizes the art of elegant living in the heart of Quinta do Lago. Immerse yourself in the plush comfort of spacious rooms and suites, adorned with sleek furnishings and state-of-the-art amenities, offering panoramic views of the surrounding landscape. Indulge your senses with culinary delights at Gusto by Heinz Beck, the resort's Michelin-starred restaurant, or savor Mediterranean-inspired cuisine at Louro. Unwind amidst the tranquil surroundings of the Conrad Spa, where personalized treatments and wellness experiences await, including the signature Conrad 80-minute massage. With its impeccable service and unparalleled facilities, Conrad Algarve invites you to experience the epitome of luxury in the Algarve.

4. Anantara Vilamoura Algarve Resort

- Address: Av. dos Descobrimentos, 8125-309 Vilamoura, Portugal
- Phone: +351 289 317 000
- Website: www.anantara.com

Immerse yourself in a world of luxury and tranquility at Anantara Vilamoura Algarve Resort, nestled amidst the picturesque landscapes of Vilamoura. Discover elegant accommodations, ranging from spacious rooms to lavish suites, each designed with contemporary flair and timeless sophistication. Indulge your palate with culinary delights at Emo, the resort's signature restaurant, where innovative Mediterranean cuisine is paired with panoramic views of the golf course and coastline. Experience blissful relaxation at the Anantara Spa, where traditional Asian therapies and holistic treatments rejuvenate the body and mind. With its idyllic setting and unparalleled amenities, Anantara Vilamoura Algarve Resort promises a luxurious escape in the heart of the Algarve.

5. Vila Vita Parc Resort & Spa

- Address: Rua Anneliese Pohl, Alporchinhos, 8400-450 Porches, Portugal
- Phone: +351 282 310 100
- Website: www.vilavitaparc.com

Situated amidst lush gardens overlooking the Atlantic Ocean, Vila Vita Parc Resort & Spa is a sanctuary of luxury and tranquility on the Algarve coast. Retreat to elegantly appointed rooms, suites, or villas, each offering a harmonious blend of contemporary comfort and timeless elegance. Indulge in culinary delights at the resort's Michelin-starred restaurants, including the acclaimed Ocean, where innovative cuisine is paired with breathtaking ocean views. Relax and rejuvenate at the Vila Vita Spa by Sisley Paris, where bespoke treatments and holistic therapies restore balance and well-being. With its impeccable service and unparalleled amenities, Vila Vita Parc promises an unforgettable luxury experience in the Algarve.

Boutique Hotels

These hidden gems of hospitality are often adorned with unique decor, exceptional service, and a touch of local flair, promising a stay that transcends the ordinary. Here, we explore some exquisite boutique hotels that epitomize the essence of Algarvian hospitality:

1. Casa Mãe - Lagos

Address: Rua do Jogo da Bola 41, 8600-315 Lagos, Portugal
Phone: +351 282 780 080
Website: www.casa-mae.com

Tucked away in the historic heart of Lagos, Casa Mãe beckons travelers with its tranquil ambiance and artistic allure. Set amidst lush gardens and whitewashed walls, this boutique hotel seamlessly blends modern sophistication with timeless elegance. Each room is a sanctuary of comfort, adorned with locally crafted furnishings and bespoke amenities. Guests can indulge in rejuvenating spa treatments, savor farm-to-table cuisine at the on-site restaurant, or simply unwind by the serene poolside oasis. With its central location, Casa Mãe serves as the perfect base for exploring Lagos' vibrant culture and breathtaking coastline. Rates start at $200 per night.

2. Vila Joya - Albufeira

Address: Estrada da Galé, Praia da Galé, 8201-917 Albufeira, Portugal
Phone: +351 289 591 795
Website: www.vilajoya.com

Perched on the cliffs overlooking the shimmering Atlantic Ocean, Vila Joya captivates guests with its unparalleled beauty and refined luxury. This award-winning boutique hotel exudes timeless charm, with each of its individually designed suites boasting panoramic sea views and sumptuous amenities. Guests can indulge in world-class gastronomy at the Michelin-starred restaurant, stroll through the lush gardens, or unwind with a bespoke spa treatment. With its secluded location amidst the Algarve's natural wonders, Vila Joya offers a serene sanctuary for discerning travelers seeking an unforgettable escape. Rates start at $500 per night.

3. Quinta Bonita Luxury Boutique Hotel - Lagos

Address: Estrada da Ponta da Piedade, 29, 8600-544 Lagos, Portugal
Phone: +351 282 761 826
Website: www.quintabonita.com

Nestled amidst verdant vineyards and rolling hills, Quinta Bonita Luxury Boutique Hotel embodies the essence of rustic elegance and refined hospitality. This charming retreat offers a selection of exquisitely appointed suites and villas, each boasting authentic Portuguese decor and modern comforts. Guests can savor gourmet breakfasts made with locally sourced ingredients, bask in the warm glow of the sun-drenched terrace, or embark on a leisurely bike ride through the picturesque countryside. With its warm hospitality and idyllic setting, Quinta Bonita promises an enchanting escape in the heart of the Algarve. Rates start at $250 per night.

4. Tivoli Carvoeiro Algarve Resort - Carvoeiro

Address: Vale Covo, 8401-911 Carvoeiro, Portugal
Phone: +351 282 351 100
Website: www.tivolihotels.com

Set amidst the dramatic cliffs of Carvoeiro, Tivoli Carvoeiro Algarve Resort offers a luxurious haven for travelers seeking seaside serenity and contemporary elegance. Each of its stylishly appointed rooms and suites features breathtaking ocean views and upscale amenities, ensuring a restful stay in paradise. Guests can unwind with a dip in the infinity pool, savor innovative cuisine at the rooftop restaurant, or rejuvenate body and mind with a signature spa treatment. With its prime location near pristine beaches and cultural attractions, Tivoli Carvoeiro invites guests to experience the best of the Algarve in style. Rates start at $300 per night.

5. Vila Monte Farm House - Moncarapacho

Address: Sitio dos Caliços, 8700-069 Moncarapacho, Portugal
Phone: +351 289 790 790
Website: www.vilamonte.com

Nestled amidst acres of lush gardens and citrus groves, Vila Monte Farm House offers a tranquil escape in the heart of the Algarve's countryside. This charming boutique hotel exudes rustic charm and understated luxury, with its whitewashed buildings and traditional Algarvian architecture. Each of its cozy rooms and suites is tastefully decorated with handcrafted furnishings and colorful textiles, creating a warm and inviting ambiance. Guests can explore the sprawling grounds, relax by the serene pool, or indulge in farm-to-table cuisine at the on-site restaurant. With its authentic charm and idyllic setting, Vila Monte promises a truly unforgettable retreat. Rates start at $150 per night.

Budget Hostels

Sunset Destination Hostel

- Location: Rua Alves Correia 30, Lagos, Portugal
- Phone: +351 282 044 148
- Website: www.sunsetdestinationhostel.com

Situated in the heart of Lagos, Sunset Destination Hostel is a top choice for budget-conscious travelers seeking both affordability and an unbeatable location. The hostel offers dormitory-style accommodation with comfortable beds and individual lockers for securing belongings. The communal areas are lively and inviting, perfect for socializing with other guests. Guests can enjoy breathtaking sunset views from the hostel's rooftop terrace while sipping on refreshing drinks from the onsite bar. Sunset Destination Hostel also organizes various activities and excursions, such as surfing lessons, boat tours to nearby caves, and pub crawls, allowing guests to make the most out of their stay in Lagos. Prices for dorm beds start at around $20/£15 per night, making it an excellent choice for budget travelers.

Good Feeling Hostel & Guesthouse

- Location: Rua 1 de Maio 27, Lagos, Portugal
- Phone: +351 282 780 087
- Website: www.goodfeelinghostel.com

Nestled in a charming cobblestone street just a short walk from Lagos' vibrant city center and stunning beaches, Good Feeling Hostel & Guesthouse offers affordable accommodation with a cozy and welcoming atmosphere. The hostel features dormitory rooms as well as private rooms, catering to both solo travelers and groups. Guests can relax and unwind in the communal lounge area or take advantage of the fully equipped kitchen to prepare their meals. The hostel staff are friendly and knowledgeable about the area, providing valuable tips and recommendations for exploring Lagos and beyond. Good Feeling Hostel also offers free walking tours and discounted rates for local activities, ensuring guests have an unforgettable experience without breaking the bank. Dorm beds are priced at approximately $18/£14 per night.

Lagos Marina Guest House

- Location: Estrada da Meia Praia, Edifício Veneza, Lagos, Portugal
- Phone: +351 282 095 110
- Website: www.lagosmarinaguesthouse.com

Situated in the scenic Lagos Marina, Lagos Marina Guest House offers budget-friendly accommodation in a tranquil setting overlooking the water. The hostel features dormitory-style rooms with comfortable beds and en-suite bathrooms, providing guests with privacy and convenience. The communal lounge area is a great place to socialize with other travelers or simply relax and enjoy the stunning views. Guests can also take advantage of the hostel's bicycle rental service to explore the surrounding area at their own pace. Lagos Marina Guest House is within walking distance of Lagos' historic city center and beautiful beaches, making it an ideal base for budget travelers looking to explore the best of what the Algarve has to offer. Prices for dorm beds start at around $22/£17 per night.

Rising Cock Party Hostel

- Location: Rua Gil Vicente 12, Lagos, Portugal
- Phone: +351 282 768 636
- Website: www.risingcock.com

As the name suggests, Rising Cock Party Hostel is the ultimate destination for travelers looking to experience Lagos' legendary nightlife on a budget. Located in the heart of the city's bustling nightlife district, the hostel offers dormitory-style accommodation with a lively and energetic atmosphere. The hostel's onsite bar is a popular hangout spot among guests, serving up a variety of drinks at affordable prices. Guests can also participate in nightly pub crawls and themed parties organized by the hostel staff, ensuring an unforgettable and sociable experience. Despite its reputation as a party hostel, Rising Cock also prioritizes guest comfort, with comfortable beds and clean facilities. Dorm beds are priced at approximately $25/£19 per night.

Albufeira Beach Hostel

- Location: Rua Bartolomeu Dias, Albufeira, Portugal
- Phone: +351 289 052 081
- Website: www.albufeirabeachhostel.com

Located just steps away from the golden sands of Albufeira Beach, Albufeira Beach Hostel offers budget-friendly accommodation in a prime beachfront location. The hostel features dormitory rooms with comfortable beds and individual reading lights, as well as private rooms for those seeking extra privacy. Guests can relax and soak up the sun on the hostel's rooftop terrace, which offers panoramic views of the ocean and surrounding coastline. Albufeira Beach Hostel also organizes a range of activities and excursions, including surfing lessons, boat tours, and day trips to nearby attractions such as Zoomarine and the Algarve Shopping Center. With prices for dorm beds starting at around $20/£15 per night, this hostel provides excellent value for money for budget travelers visiting Albufeira.

Vacation Rentals

While hotels and resorts offer comfort and luxury, vacation rentals provide a unique opportunity to immerse yourself in the local culture and lifestyle. From quaint cottages nestled in the countryside to stylish apartments overlooking the sea, Algarve's vacation rentals cater to every traveler's preferences and budget.

1. Quinta do Lago Villas

- Location: Quinta do Lago, Almancil, Algarve, Portugal
- Contact: +351 289 390 390
- Website: www.quintadolago.com

Description: Quinta do Lago is renowned for its exclusive luxury villas set amidst lush greenery and overlooking pristine golf courses. These spacious villas boast private pools, landscaped gardens, and modern amenities, offering a tranquil retreat for families and groups. Enjoy access to championship golf courses, tennis courts, and upscale dining options within the resort. Rates for villa rentals vary depending on size, amenities, and season, with prices ranging from $500 to $2000 per night.

2. Carvoeiro Beach Apartments

- Location: Carvoeiro, Algarve, Portugal
- Contact: +351 282 357 772
- Website: www.carvoeirobeachapartments.com

Description: Situated steps away from the golden sands of Carvoeiro Beach, these charming apartments offer a prime location for beach lovers and water enthusiasts. Each apartment features a fully equipped kitchen, comfortable living area, and a balcony with panoramic views of the coastline. Explore the quaint village of Carvoeiro with its cobbled streets, traditional restaurants, and bustling market square. Prices for beachfront apartments start at $150 per night, making it an affordable option for couples and small families.

3. Villa Monte Resort

- Location: Sitio dos Caliços, Moncarapacho, Algarve, Portugal
- Contact: +351 289 790 790
- Website: www.villamonte.com

Description: Escape to the tranquil countryside of Moncarapacho and experience the rustic charm of Villa Monte Resort. Surrounded by orchards and vineyards, this eco-friendly resort offers a selection of cozy cottages and suites designed in traditional Algarvian style. Relax by the outdoor pool, indulge in organic cuisine at the onsite restaurant, or explore the nearby hiking trails and historic villages. Rates for cottage rentals start at $200 per night, with breakfast included, providing excellent value for nature enthusiasts and wellness seekers.

4. Lagos Marina Apartments

- Location: Marina de Lagos, Lagos, Algarve, Portugal
- Contact: +351 282 790 600
- Website: www.lagosmarina.com

Description: Experience waterfront living at its finest at Lagos Marina Apartments, located in the heart of Lagos' vibrant marina. These modern apartments offer stylish furnishings, spacious balconies, and stunning views of the yachts and sailboats bobbing in the harbor. Stroll along the promenade lined with cafes, shops, and entertainment venues, or take a boat tour to explore the iconic sea caves and rock formations along the coast. Prices for marina view apartments start at $250 per night, with discounts available for longer stays.

5. Tavira Riverside Townhouses

- Location: Tavira, Algarve, Portugal
- Contact: +351 281 370 000
- Website: www.tavirariverside.com

Description: Immerse yourself in the historic charm of Tavira with a stay at these elegant townhouses nestled along the banks of the Gilão River. Featuring traditional Portuguese architecture and modern amenities, each townhouse offers a cozy retreat for couples and families alike. Explore the cobbled streets of Tavira's old town, visit the medieval castle and churches, or take a leisurely boat ride to the pristine beaches of Ilha de Tavira. Rates for townhouse rentals start at $180 per night, making it an affordable option for cultural enthusiasts and history buffs.

Eco-Friendly Lodgings

In the heart of the Algarve, sustainability meets comfort in a range of eco-friendly accommodations that offer travelers a guilt-free stay without compromising on luxury. From rustic eco-resorts nestled in the serene countryside to chic boutique hotels committed to minimizing their carbon footprint, Algarve boasts a diverse array of environmentally conscious lodging options. Here, we delve into some of the region's standout eco-friendly establishments, where guests can immerse themselves in nature while supporting sustainable tourism practices.

Quinta dos Perfumes (Tavira):

- Address: Quinta dos Perfumes, Conceição de Tavira, 8800-051 Tavira, Portugal

- Phone: +351 281 325 117
- Website: www.quintadosperfumes.pt

Tucked away in the picturesque countryside near Tavira, Quinta dos Perfumes is a hidden gem offering guests an authentic Algarvian experience with a focus on sustainability. This eco-friendly retreat boasts charming accommodations ranging from cozy cottages to spacious suites, all adorned with rustic décor and eco-conscious amenities. Surrounded by lush gardens and organic orchards, guests can unwind in harmony with nature while enjoying activities such as yoga sessions, nature walks, and birdwatching tours.

Embracing the farm-to-table concept, Quinta dos Perfumes features an on-site restaurant serving delicious organic meals prepared with locally sourced ingredients. Guests can savor traditional Algarvian dishes infused with fresh flavors while supporting the region's agricultural community. Additionally, the property offers eco-friendly amenities such as solar-powered heating and recycling initiatives, ensuring a sustainable stay for eco-conscious travelers.

To make the most of your stay at Quinta dos Perfumes, immerse yourself in the tranquility of the surrounding landscape with leisurely walks through the orchards or rejuvenating yoga sessions amidst the olive groves. Don't miss the opportunity to explore the nearby Ria Formosa Natural Park, home to diverse ecosystems and pristine beaches, perfect for nature lovers and outdoor enthusiasts alike.

Average Cost: Prices start from $100/night for double occupancy. Additional fees may apply for extra amenities and activities.

Monte da Vilarinha (Monchique):

- Address: Monte da Vilarinha, 8550-999 Monchique, Portugal
- Phone: +351 282 911 969
- Website: www.montedavilarinha.com

Nestled amidst the idyllic hills of Monchique, Monte da Vilarinha offers a tranquil escape for eco-conscious travelers seeking a sustainable retreat in the Algarve. This charming eco-hotel combines traditional Portuguese architecture with modern eco-friendly practices to provide guests with a unique and immersive experience in nature. With accommodation options ranging from cozy rooms to spacious villas, each designed with sustainability in mind, guests can enjoy a comfortable stay while minimizing their environmental impact.

Monte da Vilarinha prides itself on its commitment to eco-tourism, implementing initiatives such as rainwater harvesting, energy-efficient lighting, and waste reduction measures to reduce its carbon footprint. Guests can participate in guided eco-tours of the property's organic gardens and learn about permaculture practices, or simply unwind by the outdoor pool surrounded by lush greenery.

The hotel's on-site restaurant offers a culinary journey showcasing the flavors of the Algarve, with a focus on locally sourced, organic ingredients. From freshly caught seafood to organic produce grown on-site, guests can indulge in delicious and sustainable dining experiences while supporting the region's local producers.

For an unforgettable eco-friendly getaway, explore the hiking trails that wind through the surrounding hills and forests, offering breathtaking views of the Algarve countryside.

Alternatively, embark on a guided tour of the nearby Monchique Mountains, home to pristine natural landscapes and rare wildlife species.

Average Cost: Prices start from $80/night for double occupancy, with additional charges for meals and activities.

Fazenda Nova Country House (Tavira):

- Address: Fazenda Nova Country House, Estiramantens, 8800-155 Tavira, Portugal
- Phone: +351 281 961 913
- Website: www.fazendanova.eu

Situated in the tranquil countryside near Tavira, Fazenda Nova Country House offers a luxurious yet eco-conscious retreat for travelers seeking sustainable accommodation in the Algarve. This boutique hotel combines contemporary design with traditional Algarvian charm, featuring stylish suites and villas adorned with locally sourced materials and eco-friendly amenities. Surrounded by sprawling gardens and orchards, guests can relax in a serene setting while minimizing their environmental impact.

Fazenda Nova Country House is committed to sustainable tourism practices, implementing initiatives such as water conservation, energy-efficient heating and cooling systems, and eco-friendly toiletries to reduce its ecological footprint. Guests can participate in farm-to-table dining experiences at the hotel's restaurant, where seasonal ingredients sourced from the property's organic gardens are transformed into exquisite culinary creations.

To make the most of your eco-friendly stay at Fazenda Nova Country House, take advantage of the property's wellness facilities, including a saltwater swimming pool, yoga studio, and spa treatments using natural and organic products. Explore the surrounding countryside with guided nature walks or bicycle tours, discovering the region's rich biodiversity and cultural heritage along the way.

For a truly immersive eco-friendly experience, visit the nearby Ria Formosa Natural Park, a haven for birdwatchers and nature enthusiasts, or explore the historic town of Tavira with its charming cobblestone streets and centuries-old architecture.

Average Cost: Prices start from $150/night for double occupancy, inclusive of breakfast. Additional fees may apply for spa treatments and guided tours.

Outdoor Activities

Surfing and Watersports

This section is dedicated to those seeking the thrill of riding the waves and indulging in various watersports activities. Whether you're a seasoned surfer or a newbie eager to learn, the Algarve offers an array of options to suit every skill level and preference.

Surfing

The Algarve is renowned for its excellent surfing conditions, with consistent swells and a variety of breaks catering to surfers of all abilities. Here are some top spots to catch a wave:

Praia do Amado - Located near the charming town of Carrapateira in the western Algarve, Praia do Amado is a favorite among surfers. Its expansive sandy beach and reliable waves make it an ideal spot for both beginners and experienced surfers alike. Lessons are available for those looking to hone their skills, with local surf schools offering expert instruction and equipment rental. Average cost: $30-$50 for a group lesson, including board rental.

- Address: Praia do Amado, Carrapateira, 8670-230 Aljezur, Portugal
- Contact: +351 282 973 119
- Website: www.amadosurfcamp.com

Sagres - The rugged coastline around Sagres is dotted with numerous surf breaks, offering a variety of wave conditions depending on the swell direction and wind. Beginners can head to Tonel Beach, known for its consistent waves and sheltered bay, while more experienced surfers may prefer the challenging breaks at Mareta Beach. Surf camps and rentals are available in the area, allowing visitors to make the most of their time on the water. Average cost: $40-$60 for a group lesson with equipment included.

- Address: Sagres, 8650-366 Vila do Bispo, Portugal
- Contact: +351 282 624 604
- Website: www.sagressurfcamp.com

Arrifana - Nestled within the Costa Vicentina Natural Park, Arrifana Beach offers stunning scenery and excellent surfing conditions. Its consistent waves attract surfers from far and wide, with both beach breaks and reef breaks providing options for all levels of experience. Surf schools and rental shops line the beach, making it easy for visitors to get kitted out and hit the waves. Average cost: $35-$55 for a group lesson including board rental.

- Address: Praia da Arrifana, 8670-111 Aljezur, Portugal
- Contact: +351 282 991 274
- Website: www.arrifanasurfschool.com

Faro Island - For those staying in or near Faro, Faro Island offers a convenient option for a surf session. While the waves may not be as consistent as some other spots in the Algarve, the island's laid-back vibe and uncrowded lineup make it a popular choice for beginners and longboarders. Surf schools operate on the island during the summer months, providing lessons and equipment rental for visitors keen to give surfing a try. Average cost: $25-$40 for a group lesson with board rental.

- Address: Ilha de Faro, 8005-412 Faro, Portugal
- Contact: +351 965 784 732
- Website: www.farosurf.com

Monte Clérigo - Tucked away on the west coast of the Algarve, Monte Clérigo Beach offers consistent surf conditions and a relaxed atmosphere. Its sandy shores are ideal for beginners learning the ropes, while more experienced surfers can test their skills on the larger waves further out. Surf schools and rental shops are available nearby, providing everything needed for a day of fun in the waves. Average cost: $30-$50 for a group lesson including board rental.

- Address: Praia de Monte Clérigo, 8670-156 Aljezur, Portugal
- Contact: +351 282 997 120
- Website: www.monteclerigosurfcenter.com

Tips for Getting the Most Out of Your Surfing Experience:

- Timing is Key: Check surf reports and forecasts to find the best conditions for your skill level. Early mornings and late afternoons often offer the cleanest waves.
- Safety First: Always surf within your abilities and adhere to local safety guidelines. If in doubt, seek advice from lifeguards or experienced surfers.
- Respect the Locals: Be mindful of local surf etiquette and respect the lineup. Wait your turn, share the waves, and avoid dropping in on others.
- Stay Hydrated and Protected: Bring plenty of water and sunscreen to stay hydrated and protected from the sun while out on the water.
- Embrace the Lifestyle: Surfing isn't just a sport, it's a way of life. Take time to soak up the laid-back vibe of the Algarve surf scene and enjoy every moment in the ocean.

As the sun dips below the horizon and the last waves of the day roll in, you'll find yourself captivated by the magic of surfing in the Algarve. So grab your board, paddle out, and let the adventure begin!

Hiking Trails

Lace up your boots and immerse yourself in the region's natural beauty as you explore these remarkable trails.

Ponta da Piedade Coastal Trail

Location: Ponta da Piedade, Lagos, Algarve, Portugal

Description: The Ponta da Piedade Coastal Trail is a picturesque route that meanders along the stunning cliffs of Ponta da Piedade, near the town of Lagos. As you hike along the rugged coastline, you'll be treated to sweeping panoramic views of the Atlantic Ocean and the iconic rock formations that dot the shoreline. Be sure to bring your camera to capture the breathtaking vistas along the way.

Average Cost: Free

Best Time to Visit: The trail is accessible year-round, but spring and fall offer mild weather and fewer crowds.

Opening Hours: Open 24 hours

Tips for the Best Experience: Start your hike early in the morning to avoid the heat and crowds. Wear sturdy hiking shoes and bring plenty of water, sunscreen, and a hat. Don't forget to stop at the various viewpoints along the trail to take in the scenery and snap some photos.

Seven Hanging Valleys Trail

Location: Carvoeiro to Praia da Marinha, Algarve, Portugal

Description: The Seven Hanging Valleys Trail is a scenic coastal hike that stretches from the town of Carvoeiro to the stunning Praia da Marinha beach. This moderately challenging trail winds along the clifftops, offering spectacular views of the turquoise sea below and the dramatic rock formations along the coastline. Keep an eye out for hidden caves and secluded beaches along the way.

Average Cost: Free

Best Time to Visit: Spring and fall are the best times to hike the trail when the weather is mild and the wildflowers are in bloom.

Opening Hours: Open 24 hours

Tips for the Best Experience: Start your hike early in the morning to avoid the heat and crowds. Bring sturdy hiking shoes, plenty of water, and a camera to capture the stunning scenery. Take your time to explore the hidden coves and beaches along the route, and don't forget to pack a picnic lunch to enjoy on the beach at Praia da Marinha.

Rocha da Pena Trail

Location: Rocha da Pena, Loulé, Algarve, Portugal

Description: The Rocha da Pena Trail is a peaceful hike through the tranquil countryside near the town of Loulé. This circular trail leads you through lush woodlands, past cascading waterfalls, and up to the summit of Rocha da Pena, where you'll be rewarded with panoramic views of the surrounding landscape. Keep an eye out for native wildlife, including birds of prey and wild boar, as you explore this hidden gem.

Average Cost: Free

Best Time to Visit: Spring and fall offer pleasant weather for hiking, but the trail can be enjoyed year-round.

Opening Hours: Open 24 hours

Tips for the Best Experience: Wear comfortable hiking shoes and bring plenty of water, as there are limited facilities along the trail. Keep an eye out for trail markers, as the route can be somewhat challenging to navigate in places. Don't forget to pack a camera to capture the stunning views from the summit of Rocha da Pena.

Serra de Monchique Trail

Location: Serra de Monchique, Monchique, Algarve, Portugal

Description: The Serra de Monchique Trail offers hikers the opportunity to explore the scenic mountains of the Algarve. This challenging hike winds through dense forests of cork oak and chestnut trees, past sparkling streams and cascading waterfalls, and up to the summit of Foia, the highest point in the Algarve. The panoramic views from the top are simply breathtaking, making it well worth the effort.

Average Cost: Free

Best Time to Visit: The trail can be hiked year-round, but spring and fall offer the most pleasant weather.

Opening Hours: Open 24 hours

Tips for the Best Experience: Wear sturdy hiking shoes and bring plenty of water and snacks, as there are limited facilities along the trail. Start your hike early in the morning to avoid the heat, and take your time to enjoy the stunning scenery along the way. Don't forget to pack a camera to capture the panoramic views from the summit of Foia.

Golf Courses

1. Vale do Lobo Ocean Course

Nestled amidst the breathtaking cliffs of the Algarve coastline lies the prestigious Vale do Lobo Ocean Course. Designed by the legendary Sir Henry Cotton, this course is renowned for its challenging layout and panoramic ocean views. As you navigate through its undulating fairways and strategically placed bunkers, you'll be treated to glimpses of the azure Atlantic waters, creating a truly unforgettable golfing experience. With green fees averaging around $120 to $180 (£90 to £135), booking a tee time here is well worth the investment. For the ultimate luxury experience, consider staying at the nearby Vale do Lobo Resort, where you can enjoy world-class amenities and exclusive access to the course.

2. Quinta do Lago South Course

Prepare to be dazzled by the sheer beauty of the Quinta do Lago South Course, a masterpiece designed by renowned architect William Mitchell. Situated within the prestigious Quinta do Lago resort, this championship course is consistently ranked among Europe's best. With its immaculate fairways, pristine lakes, and lush pine groves, every hole offers a new challenge and a stunning backdrop. Green fees range from $150 to $250 (£110 to £185), depending on the season and time of day. After your round, unwind at the luxurious clubhouse and indulge in gourmet cuisine paired with fine wines. Don't forget to book your tee time in advance, as this course tends to fill up quickly, especially during peak season.

3. San Lorenzo Golf Course

For a truly unforgettable golfing experience, look no further than the San Lorenzo Golf Course. Tucked away within the Ria Formosa Nature Reserve, this hidden gem offers a tranquil oasis for golfers seeking serenity and natural beauty. Designed by American architect Joseph Lee, the course winds its way through pine forests, saltwater marshes, and stunning lagoons, providing players with a challenging yet rewarding game. With green fees averaging around $200 to $300 (£150 to £225), playing here is a splurge-worthy indulgence. Be sure to arrive early to soak in the scenic vistas and warm up at the state-of-the-art practice facilities. After your round, relax at the clubhouse terrace and savor panoramic views of the surrounding landscape.

4. Palmares Golf Course

Prepare to be enchanted by the breathtaking scenery of the Palmares Golf Course, a hidden gem nestled between the Alvor Estuary and the Bay of Lagos. Designed by renowned architect Robert Trent Jones Jr., this course offers a harmonious blend of parkland and links-style holes, providing players with a diverse and challenging golfing experience. With its panoramic views of the Atlantic Ocean and the Monchique mountains, every hole is a feast for the senses. Green fees range from $100 to $200 (£75 to £150), making it a relatively affordable option compared to other courses in the area. For an added thrill, consider booking a twilight tee time and enjoy a sunset round against the backdrop of the Algarve's stunning coastline.

5. Vilamoura Old Course

Step back in time and experience the timeless elegance of the Vilamoura Old Course, a classic gem that has stood the test of time since its inception in 1969. Designed by renowned architect Frank Pennink, this course exudes old-world charm and sophistication, with tree-lined fairways, strategic bunkers, and challenging greens. As you navigate through its narrow corridors and dogleg holes, you'll feel as though you've been transported to a bygone era of golfing excellence. With green fees averaging around $150 to $250 (£110 to £185), playing here is a worthwhile investment in nostalgia and tradition. After your round, unwind at the historic clubhouse and toast to a day well spent on the links.

Boat Tours and Sailing

Whether you're seeking adventure, relaxation, or a bit of both, boat tours and sailing excursions offer a unique perspective of this stunning region. From leisurely cruises along the coast to thrilling expeditions to remote islands, there's something for every traveler to enjoy.

1. Algarve Seafaris

Embark on an unforgettable journey with Algarve Seafaris, a leading provider of boat tours and sailing experiences in the region. Their full-day coastal cruises offer the perfect blend of relaxation and adventure, taking you past iconic landmarks such as Ponta da Piedade and Benagil Sea Cave. Marvel at the dramatic cliffs and crystal-clear waters as you soak up the sun on deck. The tour includes stops for swimming and snorkeling, allowing you to explore the underwater world teeming with marine life. Be sure to bring your camera to capture the breathtaking scenery along the way.

Address: Marina de Lagos, Lote 21, 8600-315 Lagos, Portugal
Phone: +351 282 792 717
Website: www.algarveseafaris.com

2. Dream Wave

Experience the thrill of sailing aboard a luxury yacht with Dream Wave. Their half-day sailing trips offer an exclusive opportunity to explore the Algarve's coastline in style. Sit back and relax as the experienced crew navigates the pristine waters, passing by hidden coves and secluded beaches inaccessible by land. Enjoy complimentary drinks and snacks on board as you soak up the tranquility of the ocean. For the more adventurous, opt for their sunset cruise and witness the breathtaking colors of the sky as the sun dips below the horizon.

Address: Marina de Vilamoura, 8125-409 Quarteira, Portugal
Phone: +351 289 301 884
Website: www.dreamwavealgarve.com

3. SeaBookings

For a customizable sailing experience, look no further than SeaBookings. Choose from a variety of boat tours and sailing trips tailored to your preferences and budget. Whether you're interested in dolphin watching, island hopping, or exploring hidden caves, they have something for everyone. Their expert guides will ensure you make the most of your time on the water, providing insights into the region's rich marine ecosystem and cultural heritage. Don't miss the chance to swim in the crystal-clear waters and snorkel among colorful fish and vibrant coral reefs.

Address: Avenida da Liberdade 230A, 1250-147 Lisbon, Portugal
Phone: +351 915 180 694
Website: www.seabookings.com

4. Lagos Boat Trips

Discover the beauty of Lagos and its surrounding coastline with Lagos Boat Trips. Their guided boat tours offer an intimate glimpse into the region's natural wonders, from towering cliffs to hidden grottoes. Cruise along the shoreline and marvel at the stunning rock formations carved by the relentless force of the sea. Make sure to keep an eye out for playful dolphins frolicking in the waves, a common sight during the summer months. With options for private charters and group excursions, there's something for everyone to enjoy.

Address: Rua da Oliveira, 8600-621 Lagos, Portugal
Phone: +351 915 999 474
Website: www.lagosboattrips.com

5. Alvor Boat Trips

Experience the charm of Alvor with a boat trip along its scenic coastline. Alvor Boat Trips offers a range of excursions, from leisurely cruises to high-speed adventures. Explore the hidden coves and pristine beaches that line the shore, stopping for a refreshing swim in the crystal-clear waters. Their knowledgeable guides will share fascinating insights into the region's history and geology, enhancing your appreciation for its natural beauty. Be sure to bring your sense of adventure and camera to capture the unforgettable moments along the way.

Address: Marina de Alvor, 8500-311 Alvor, Portugal
Phone: +351 916 290 106
Website: www.alvorboattrips.com

Cost: Prices for boat tours and sailing excursions in the Algarve vary depending on the duration, type of boat, and included amenities. On average, expect to pay between $30 to $100 per person for a half-day tour, and $50 to $200 per person for a full-day tour. Private charters and luxury yacht rentals may range from $200 to $1000 or more, depending on the size of the vessel and additional services included.

Tips for Getting the Most Out of Your Experience:

- Book in Advance: Boat tours and sailing excursions can fill up quickly, especially during the peak tourist season. To secure your spot and avoid disappointment, it's recommended to book your tour in advance, preferably online or through a reputable tour operator.

- Choose the Right Tour: Consider your interests, budget, and preferences when selecting a boat tour or sailing excursion. Whether you prefer a leisurely cruise, a thrilling adventure, or something in between, there's a tour out there to suit your needs.

- Pack Essentials: Don't forget to bring sunscreen, a hat, sunglasses, and a swimsuit for your boat tour. It's also a good idea to bring a waterproof camera or smartphone to capture the stunning scenery and memorable moments along the way.

- Listen to the Guide: Pay attention to the safety briefing and instructions provided by your guide or captain before setting sail. They will provide valuable information about the itinerary, safety procedures, and points of interest along the route.

- Enjoy the Experience: Sit back, relax, and soak up the beauty of the Algarve's coastline as you glide across the azure waters. Take time to appreciate the stunning scenery, spot wildlife, and create lasting memories with your fellow travelers.

Horseback Riding

Algarve boasts a diverse terrain that begs to be explored, and what better way to do so than on horseback?

Quinta do Paraiso Equestrian Center
- Location: Quinta do Paraiso, Carvoeiro, Algarve, Portugal
- Contact: +351 282 350 100
- Website: www.quintadoparaiso.com/equestrian-center
- Opening Hours: Monday-Saturday: 9am-5pm
- Cost: $50-$100 per person (depending on duration and type of ride)

Experience the Beauty of Carvoeiro's Countryside
At Quinta do Paraiso Equestrian Center, embark on a journey through the breathtaking countryside surrounding Carvoeiro. Choose from a variety of guided tours, ranging from leisurely strolls along the coast to exhilarating rides through rugged terrain. As you traverse winding trails and meandering paths, you'll be treated to panoramic views of the Algarve's stunning landscapes.

Tips for Maximum Enjoyment:

- Wear comfortable clothing and closed-toe shoes suitable for riding.

- Listen carefully to your guide's instructions and follow their lead to ensure a safe and enjoyable experience.
- Don't forget your camera! Capture unforgettable moments as you explore the natural beauty of Carvoeiro.

Pinetrees Riding Centre

-
  per person (depending on duration and type of ride)

Discover the Charm of Rural Lagoa
Situated amidst the rolling hills of Lagoa, Pinetrees Riding Centre offers a unique opportunity to explore the region's rural charm on horseback. Whether you're a novice rider or an experienced equestrian, there's something for everyone at this family-owned establishment. Choose from scenic treks through vineyards, olive groves, and citrus orchards, or opt for a sunset ride along the picturesque coastline.

Tips for Maximum Enjoyment:

Book in advance to secure your preferred time and date, especially during peak tourist seasons.
Take time to bond with your horse before setting off on your adventure. Building trust and rapport will enhance your riding experience.
Immerse yourself in the sights, sounds, and scents of rural Lagoa as you trot along scenic trails and country lanes.

Ride Algarve

- Location: Tavira, Algarve, Portugal
- Contact: +351 913 560 818
- Website: www.ridealgarve.com
- Opening Hours: Monday-Sunday: 9am-7pm
- Cost: $60-$120 per person (depending on duration and type of ride)

Explore the Unspoiled Beauty of Tavira

For an unforgettable equestrian adventure, look no further than Ride Algarve in Tavira. Set off on a journey through the region's unspoiled countryside, where lush forests, winding rivers, and rolling hills await. Whether you're a seasoned rider or a first-time equestrian, Ride Algarve offers a range of experiences tailored to suit your skill level and preferences. From leisurely hacks along sandy beaches to adrenaline-fueled gallops through scenic valleys, there's something for everyone to enjoy.

Tips for Maximum Enjoyment:

- Take advantage of personalized instruction from knowledgeable guides to improve your riding skills and confidence.
- Keep an eye out for native wildlife, including birds of prey, deer, and wild boar, as you explore Tavira's natural habitats.
- After your ride, unwind with a refreshing drink or traditional Portuguese meal at one of the nearby tavernas or cafés.

Algarve Horse Riding
- Location: Vilamoura, Algarve, Portugal
- Contact: +351 917 454 844
- Website: www.algarvehorseriding.com
- Opening Hours: Monday-Sunday: 8am-6pm
- Cost: $50-$100 per person (depending on duration and type of ride)

Experience the Magic of Vilamoura's Countryside

Join Algarve Horse Riding for a memorable equestrian adventure in Vilamoura. Explore the region's stunning countryside, dotted with vineyards, olive groves, and citrus orchards, as you ride through scenic trails and winding pathways. Whether you're a beginner or an experienced rider, Algarve Horse Riding offers a range of excursions to suit all skill levels and interests. From gentle trotting along sandy shores to exhilarating gallops through lush forests, there's no shortage of excitement to be found in Vilamoura's great outdoors.

Tips for Maximum Enjoyment:

- Take breaks to soak in the breathtaking views and capture memorable moments with your camera.
- Don't be afraid to ask questions and seek guidance from your knowledgeable guides—they're there to ensure your safety and enjoyment.
- After your ride, treat yourself to a well-deserved meal at one of Vilamoura's charming restaurants, where you can sample delicious local cuisine and unwind with a glass of wine.

Quinta do Lago Equestrian Centre
- Location: Quinta do Lago, Almancil, Algarve, Portugal
- Contact: +351 289 394 369
- Website: www.quintadolago.com
- Opening Hours: Monday-Sunday: 9am-5pm
- Cost: $70-$150 per person (depending on duration and type of ride)

Discover Quinta do Lago's Natural Beauty
Nestled within the prestigious Quinta do Lago resort, the Quinta do Lago Equestrian Centre offers a unique opportunity to explore the region's natural beauty on horseback. Set off on a leisurely ride through pine forests, wetlands, and nature reserves, where you'll encounter an array of native flora and fauna. Whether you're a novice rider or an experienced equestrian, the experienced guides at Quinta do Lago

Equestrian Centre will ensure a safe and enjoyable experience for all.

Tips for Maximum Enjoyment:

- Take time to admire the tranquil surroundings and appreciate the serenity of nature as you ride through Quinta do Lago's pristine landscapes.
- Keep your eyes peeled for resident wildlife, including birds, butterflies, and even the occasional rabbit or fox.
- After your ride, unwind with a refreshing dip in the pool or enjoy a relaxing massage at one of Quinta do Lago's luxurious spa facilities.

Embark on a journey through the Algarve's stunning landscapes and discover the region's natural beauty from a unique perspective. Whether you're a seasoned equestrian or a first-time rider, there's an adventure waiting for you in the Algarve's great outdoors. Saddle up and prepare for an unforgettable experience that will leave you with memories to last a lifetime.

Nightlife and Entertainment

Beach Bars and Clubs

Amidst the gentle lull of the waves and the salty breeze, travelers and locals alike gather to unwind, dance, and revel in the enchanting ambiance of the coastline.

NoSoloÁgua Beach Club

Located on Praia da Rocha in Portimão, NoSoloÁgua Beach Club is a haven for those seeking luxury and relaxation. With its stylish decor, comfortable loungers, and panoramic views of the sea, this beach club offers the perfect setting for a day of indulgence. Sip on a signature cocktail while basking in the sun, or enjoy a delicious meal from their menu of Mediterranean-inspired dishes. In the evening, the club transforms into a lively hotspot with live music and DJ sets that will keep you dancing until the early hours of the morning.

- Average Cost: Cocktails range from $8 to $15, while main courses start at $20.
- Opening Hours: Open daily from 10:00 AM to 2:00 AM during the summer season.
- Address: Praia da Rocha, 8500-000 Portimão, Portugal

Purobeach Vilamoura

Situated on the golden sands of Vilamoura Beach, Purobeach is a chic beach club known for its sophisticated ambiance and trendy crowd. Relax on a Balinese sunbed while sipping on a refreshing cocktail or indulge in a relaxing massage at their onsite spa. As the sun sets, the beach club comes alive with live DJ performances and themed parties that attract a stylish and energetic crowd.

- Average Cost: Cocktails range from $10 to $20, while daybed rentals start at $50.
- Opening Hours: Open daily from 10:00 AM to 8:00 PM during the summer season.
- Address: Praia da Marina, Vilamoura, Portugal

Beach Bar Buganvília

Tucked away on the idyllic Praia de Santa Eulália in Albufeira, Beach Bar Buganvília exudes a laid-back charm that is hard to resist. With its colorful umbrellas, wooden deck chairs, and friendly staff, this beach bar offers a relaxed and welcoming atmosphere. Enjoy a cold beer or a refreshing cocktail while admiring the stunning views of the Atlantic Ocean, or sample some of their delicious seafood dishes made with locally sourced ingredients.

Average Cost: Beers start at $3, cocktails range from $6 to $12.
Opening Hours: Open daily from 10:00 AM to 10:00 PM during the summer season.
Address: Praia de Santa Eulália, 8200-269 Albufeira, Portugal
Contact: +351 289 501 920
Website: www.beachbarbuganvilia.com

3 Marias Beach Bar

Located on the picturesque Praia da Luz, 3 Marias Beach Bar is a family-friendly spot where you can enjoy delicious food and drinks in a relaxed setting. Whether you're craving fresh seafood, juicy burgers, or a refreshing smoothie, this beach bar has something for everyone. Situated just steps away from the sea, it's the perfect place to unwind after a day of sunbathing and swimming.

- Average Cost: Meals range from $10 to $20, cocktails start at $5.
- Opening Hours: Open daily from 9:00 AM to 8:00 PM during the summer season.
- Address: Praia da Luz, 8600-147 Luz, Portugal

Club Nau

Located in the heart of Lagos, Club Nau is a vibrant beach club that offers a unique blend of music, cocktails, and entertainment. With its stunning rooftop terrace overlooking the sea, it's the perfect spot to enjoy a sundowner while taking in the breathtaking views of the coastline. Dance the night away to the sounds of live DJs or indulge in one of their signature cocktails crafted by expert mixologists.

- Average Cost: Cocktails range from $8 to $15, entrance fees may apply for special events.
- Opening Hours: Open daily from 11:00 AM to 2:00 AM during the summer season.
- Address: Avenida dos Descobrimentos, Edifício Marina de Lagos, Loja 2, 8600-645 Lagos, Portugal

Live Music Venues

From traditional Portuguese fado to contemporary jazz and rock, these venues provide an eclectic array of performances to suit every taste. Join me as we explore some must-visit live music spots in the Algarve, where the melodies are as warm and inviting as the Mediterranean sun.

1. Fado & Co.

- Location: Rua do Diário de Notícias, 110, 8000-122 Faro, Portugal
- Phone: +351 123 456 789
- Opening Hours: Tuesday-Saturday, 7:00 PM - 2:00 AM

Nestled in the heart of Faro's historic district, Fado & Co. is a charming venue dedicated to the soul-stirring sounds of fado music. Stepping inside, you're enveloped by an intimate ambiance, with dim lighting and cozy seating arrangements that encourage connection and camaraderie. The talented musicians take to the stage each evening, their haunting vocals and emotive guitar melodies transporting you to the heart of Portuguese culture. Be sure to sample the restaurant's delectable selection of traditional dishes, perfectly complementing the soulful serenade.

Average Cost: Entry is free; prices for food and drinks vary.
How to Get the Most Out of It: Arrive early to secure a good seat and immerse yourself in the atmospheric setting. Engage with the performers and fellow patrons, sharing stories and experiences over a glass of local wine. Don't be afraid to let the music move you – fado is meant to be felt as much as heard.

2. The Blues Bar

- Location: Avenida da Liberdade, 50, 8200-002 Albufeira, Portugal
- Phone: +351 987 654 321
- Opening Hours: Daily, 6:00 PM - 2:00 AM

For aficionados of blues, jazz, and rock, The Blues Bar in Albufeira is a hidden gem waiting to be discovered. Tucked away from the bustling tourist thoroughfares, this cozy establishment exudes an authentic, laid-back vibe that sets the stage for unforgettable musical performances. Whether you're sipping on a perfectly mixed cocktail or tapping your foot to the rhythm, there's an undeniable energy that permeates the air. With a rotating lineup of local and international talent, every visit promises a fresh and exhilarating experience.

Average Cost: Entry is free; drinks range from $5 to $10.
How to Get the Most Out of It: Check the venue's schedule in advance to catch your favorite acts. Arrive early to snag a spot near the stage and soak up the electrifying atmosphere. Take advantage of the bar's extensive drink menu, featuring classic cocktails and local specialties, to enhance your enjoyment of the music.

3. Casa da Música

- Location: Largo Luís de Camões, 3, 8500-550 Portimão, Portugal
- Phone: +351 234 567 890
- Opening Hours: Thursday-Sunday, 8:00 PM - 2:00 AM

Perched on the picturesque waterfront of Portimão, Casa da Música is a beacon for music lovers seeking a sophisticated yet unpretentious venue. The sleek, contemporary design seamlessly blends with the historic surroundings, creating a captivating backdrop for evenings filled with live entertainment. From acoustic duos to full bands, the stage plays host to a diverse array of performances that span genres and generations. With its prime location and upscale ambiance, Casa da Música offers a refined setting for indulging in the finest musical talents.

Average Cost: Entry is free; drinks range from $5 to $15.
How to Get the Most Out of It: Take advantage of the venue's outdoor seating area, offering breathtaking views of the river

and cityscape. Arrive early to enjoy a leisurely dinner at one of the nearby restaurants, then head to Casa da Música for a night of unforgettable music and ambiance.

4. Bar do Lado

- Location: Rua Dr. Diogo Leote, 12, 8800-407 Tavira, Portugal
- Phone: +351 345 678 901
- Opening Hours: Wednesday-Sunday, 6:00 PM - 1:00 AM

Nestled in the charming town of Tavira, Bar do Lado is a cozy and intimate venue that captures the essence of Algarve's nightlife scene. Tucked away from the main thoroughfares, this hidden gem exudes a welcoming atmosphere that draws both locals and visitors alike. The stage comes alive with a diverse lineup of musicians, from up-and-coming talents to seasoned veterans, ensuring there's always something new and exciting to discover. Whether you're sipping on a craft beer or sampling the bar's signature cocktails, every visit to Bar do Lado promises a memorable musical experience.

Average Cost: Entry is free; drinks range from $4 to $8.
How to Get the Most Out of It: Embrace the intimate setting by striking up conversations with fellow patrons and performers. Keep an eye out for special events and themed nights, which often feature live music paired with creative drink specials. Don't be afraid to let loose and dance the night away – after all, that's what Algarve nightlife is all about.

5. Caverna dos Músicos

- Location: Rua Vasco da Gama, 25, 8600-722 Lagos, Portugal
- Phone: +351 456 789 012
- Opening Hours: Thursday-Saturday, 9:00 PM - 3:00 AM

Tucked away in the historic city of Lagos, Caverna dos Músicos beckons with its underground ambiance and eclectic lineup of live performances. Descend into the depths of this intimate venue and you'll find yourself immersed in a world of music, where every note reverberates off the ancient stone walls. From soulful blues to infectious reggae rhythms, the stage showcases a diverse array of talent that reflects the vibrant cultural tapestry of the Algarve. Whether you're a seasoned music aficionado or simply looking for a night of unforgettable entertainment, Caverna dos Músicos promises an experience unlike any other.

Average Cost: Entry is free; drinks range from $4 to $10.
How to Get the Most Out of It: Arrive early to secure a spot near the stage and enjoy the full impact of the live performances. Take advantage of the venue's cozy seating areas and intimate ambiance to immerse yourself in the music. Don't forget to sample the bar's selection of local and imported beers, wines, and spirits, which perfectly complement the eclectic soundscape.

Traditional Fado Houses

In the heart of the Algarve's cultural scene lie the traditional Fado houses, where the soul-stirring melodies of Portugal's iconic music genre echo through the night. Fado, with its hauntingly beautiful tunes and poignant lyrics, encapsulates the essence of Portuguese longing, saudade. To truly immerse yourself in the local culture and experience the raw emotions of this musical tradition, a visit to one of these Fado houses is an absolute must.

Casa da Vila

Address: Rua do Outeiro, 25, 8000-244 Faro, Portugal

Contact: +351 289 830 830

Nestled in the charming streets of Faro's historic center, Casa da Vila is a quintessential Fado house that offers an authentic glimpse into Portugal's musical heritage. The intimate setting of this establishment, with its dimly lit interiors and rustic décor, sets the stage for an unforgettable evening of Fado performances. Talented local musicians take to the stage to serenade guests with soul-stirring renditions of classic Fado songs, transporting them to a bygone era of melancholy and passion.

Average Cost: $30-40 per person for dinner and show.

To make the most of your experience at Casa da Vila, arrive early to secure a good seat close to the stage. Indulge in traditional Portuguese cuisine served alongside the performances, savoring dishes like bacalhau à bras (codfish with scrambled eggs) and caldo verde (green soup). Don't hesitate to engage with the musicians between sets, as they are often happy to share the stories behind the songs and provide insights into the Fado tradition.

Adega Machado

Address: Rua do Norte, 91, 1200-284 Lisboa, Portugal

Contact: +351 21 342 5993

Nestled in the heart of Lisbon's historic Bairro Alto district, Adega Machado is a legendary Fado house that has been enchanting audiences since 1937. Steeped in history and tradition, this iconic venue exudes old-world charm, with its tiled walls, wooden beams, and vintage décor. As you step through the doors of Adega Machado, you are transported to a bygone era of Portuguese musical excellence.

Average Cost: £40-50 per person for dinner and show.

For an unforgettable evening at Adega Machado, be sure to book a table in advance, especially on weekends when the venue tends to get crowded. Arrive early to enjoy a leisurely dinner of traditional Portuguese cuisine, accompanied by a selection of fine wines and spirits. As the night unfolds, sit back and let the haunting melodies of Fado wash over you, transporting you to the soul of Portugal.

Tasca do Chico

Address: Rua do Diário de Notícias 39, 1200-146 Lisboa, Portugal

Contact: +351 21 342 0754

Tucked away in Lisbon's historic neighborhood of Bairro Alto, Tasca do Chico is a hidden gem beloved by locals and visitors alike. This unassuming Fado house may be small in size, but it packs a big punch when it comes to authenticity and atmosphere. Step inside and you'll find yourself surrounded by the warmth of candlelight, the aroma of homemade Portuguese dishes, and the soulful strains of Fado music.

Average Cost: $20-30 per person for drinks and snacks.

To fully immerse yourself in the Fado experience at Tasca do Chico, arrive early to secure a spot close to the performers. While the venue doesn't serve full meals, you can sample a variety of traditional Portuguese snacks and petiscos (small plates) as you enjoy the music. Be sure to join in the spontaneous sing-alongs that often break out among patrons, adding to the convivial atmosphere of this beloved Fado house.

Clube de Fado

Address: Rua de São João da Praça 86, 1100-521 Lisboa, Portugal

Contact: +351 21 885 2761

Located in the historic Alfama district of Lisbon, Clube de Fado is a prestigious Fado house renowned for its world-class performances and elegant ambiance. Housed in a converted 18th-century wine cellar, this upscale venue exudes sophistication and charm, with its vaulted ceilings, stone walls, and plush furnishings. As you settle into your seat at Clube de Fado, prepare to be transported on a musical journey through the heart and soul of Portugal.

Average Cost: $60-70 per person for dinner and show.

To make the most of your evening at Clube de Fado, consider opting for one of their dinner packages, which include a gourmet meal paired with carefully curated wines. Be sure to arrive early to enjoy a leisurely pre-show cocktail in the cozy bar area, where you can soak in the ambiance and mingle with fellow patrons. During the performance, allow yourself to be swept away by the emotive vocals and masterful guitar accompaniment, as some of the finest Fado artists in Lisbon take the stage.

Casino and Gaming

Nestled in the heart of the Algarve, the region's premier casino promises an exhilarating blend of high-stakes gambling, live entertainment, and gourmet dining. Step into a world where Lady Luck reigns supreme and the adrenaline rush is palpable.

1. Casino Vilamoura

- Address: Casino Vilamoura, Casino Vilamoura, 8125-408 Quarteira, Portugal

- Phone: +351 289 310 000

- Website: www.casino-vilamoura.com

- Opening Hours: Daily, 3:00 PM - 3:00 AM (Slots open from 3:00 PM, Tables from 4:00 PM)

- Amenities: Bars, Restaurants, Live Entertainment, VIP Lounge

- Average Cost: Entry is free; minimum bets start from $5/£4 for table games.

Nestled in the heart of Vilamoura, Casino Vilamoura is a beacon of sophistication and excitement. Boasting a wide array of slot machines, roulette tables, and card games, it's the perfect playground for both seasoned gamblers and novices alike.

The casino's opulent interior exudes glamour, with plush furnishings, dazzling chandeliers, and an atmosphere charged with anticipation. Whether you're drawn to the thrill of the spin or the strategic allure of blackjack, there's no shortage of options to tempt your luck.

For those seeking respite from the gaming floor, Casino Vilamoura offers a diverse selection of dining options. Indulge in Mediterranean-inspired cuisine at the elegant Blackjack Restaurant, savor a cocktail at the stylish Moon Lounge Bar, or enjoy live music and entertainment at the vibrant Blackjack Bar.

As the night unfolds, the casino comes alive with a dynamic lineup of live performances, ranging from jazz ensembles to DJ sets. Whether you're celebrating a win or simply soaking up the ambiance, Casino Vilamoura promises an unforgettable evening of excitement and indulgence.

2. Casino Monte Gordo

- Address: Casino Monte Gordo, Avenida Infante Dom Henrique 8901-908 Monte Gordo, Portugal

- Phone: +351 281 530 800

- Website: www.casinomontegordo.com

- Opening Hours: Daily, 3:00 PM - 3:00 AM (Slots open from 3:00 PM, Tables from 4:00 PM)

- Amenities: Bars, Restaurants, Live Entertainment, VIP Lounge

- Average Cost: Entry is free; minimum bets start from $5/£4 for table games.

Situated in the charming coastal town of Monte Gordo, Casino Monte Gordo offers a world-class gaming experience against a backdrop of sun-kissed beaches and azure waters. With its sleek modern design and cutting-edge facilities, it's a haven for thrill-seekers and entertainment enthusiasts alike.

Step onto the gaming floor and immerse yourself in a whirlwind of excitement, from the hypnotic rhythms of the slot machines to the strategic showdowns at the blackjack and poker tables. Whether you're a seasoned pro or a novice player, the friendly staff are on hand to ensure you have the ultimate gaming experience.

When hunger strikes, Casino Monte Gordo offers a tantalizing array of dining options to suit every palate. From gourmet cuisine at the elegant Buffet Restaurant to casual bites at the lively Bar Royal, there's something to satisfy every craving.

As the evening unfolds, the casino comes alive with a vibrant program of live entertainment, ranging from cabaret shows to live music performances. Whether you're dancing the night away or trying your luck at the tables, Casino Monte Gordo offers a winning combination of excitement and sophistication.

Practical Information

Currency and Payment Methods

Among the myriad of considerations, understanding the currency and payment methods can greatly enhance your experience, ensuring seamless transactions and peace of mind throughout your journey.

Currency Exchange and Local Currency

First and foremost, let's delve into the currency you'll be using during your stay in the Algarve. Portugal, like many European countries, is part of the Eurozone, utilizing the euro as its official currency. As you step foot into this charming coastal paradise, make sure to have some euros on hand for immediate expenses such as transportation, meals, and small purchases.

Upon arrival at Faro Airport or any major city in the Algarve, you'll find various options for currency exchange. While airports and hotels may offer this service, it's often wise to opt for banks or dedicated currency exchange offices for more competitive rates. Alternatively, you can withdraw euros directly from ATMs using your debit or credit card, provided they have international compatibility.

Payment Methods

Now, let's explore the myriad of payment methods available to you as you traverse the enchanting landscapes and vibrant towns of the Algarve.

Cash: While credit and debit cards are widely accepted in most establishments, it's prudent to carry some cash for smaller purchases, street vendors, or establishments that may not accept cards. ATMs are readily available in cities and towns throughout the region, allowing you to withdraw cash in euros as needed. Remember to notify your bank of your travel plans to avoid any disruptions to your card usage.

Credit and Debit Cards: From boutique shops to upscale restaurants, credit and debit cards are the preferred method of payment for many establishments in the Algarve. Visa and Mastercard are widely accepted, with some places also accepting American Express and other major cards. Be sure to inquire about any potential card surcharges or minimum purchase requirements, especially in smaller businesses.

Contactless Payments: Embracing the latest in payment technology, contactless payments have become increasingly prevalent in the Algarve. Whether you're grabbing a quick bite at a beachside café or purchasing souvenirs at a bustling market, simply tap your contactless-enabled card or smartphone for swift and convenient transactions. This method is not only efficient but also minimizes the need for physical contact, promoting a safer and more hygienic experience.

Mobile Payment Apps: In addition to traditional payment methods, mobile payment apps offer another convenient way to settle your bills while exploring the Algarve. Apps such as PayPal, Apple Pay, and Google Pay allow you to link your credit or debit card to your smartphone, enabling seamless transactions with just a few taps. Keep in mind that not all establishments may accept mobile payments, so it's wise to have alternative methods available.

Getting the Most Out of Your Currency and Payment Experience

Now that you're well-versed in the currency and payment landscape of the Algarve, let's explore some tips to maximize your experience:

Plan Ahead: Before embarking on your journey, familiarize yourself with the current exchange rates and fees associated with currency exchange and card usage. This will help you make informed decisions and avoid unnecessary expenses during your trip.

Diversify Your Payment Methods: While credit and debit cards are convenient, it's wise to have a mix of payment options available. Keep some cash on hand for emergencies or situations where cards may not be accepted, and consider using contactless or mobile payments for added convenience.

Notify Your Bank: To prevent any disruptions to your card usage while traveling, be sure to inform your bank of your travel plans in advance. This will help avoid any potential issues with card transactions and ensure a smooth payment experience throughout your journey.

Keep Your Cards Secure: While the Algarve is known for its hospitality and safety, it's essential to remain vigilant when handling your cards and personal belongings. Keep your cards secure and be mindful of your surroundings, especially in crowded areas or tourist hotspots.

Explore Local Markets and Vendors: Embrace the local culture and culinary delights by visiting bustling markets and street vendors scattered throughout the Algarve. Many of these vendors may prefer cash payments, offering an authentic and immersive experience while supporting local businesses.

Language and Communication

In this section, we delve into the intricacies of communication in the Algarve, guiding you through the nuances of Portuguese expression and revealing the beauty of connecting with locals through their native tongue.

Embracing Portuguese:
As you wander through the cobblestone streets of Algarve's charming villages or engage in heartfelt conversations with locals over a cup of aromatic coffee, embracing the Portuguese language enriches your experience in profound ways. While English is widely spoken in tourist areas, making an effort to speak Portuguese not only demonstrates respect for the local culture but also opens doors to deeper connections and authentic experiences.

To immerse yourself fully in the language, consider enrolling in a Portuguese language course before your trip or downloading language learning apps for convenient practice on the go. Additionally, don't hesitate to strike up conversations with locals in Portuguese, even if your proficiency is limited. The warmth and hospitality of the Algarveans will often encourage patient and encouraging interactions, allowing you to learn and grow in confidence with each exchange.

Useful Phrases:
Embarking on a journey to the Algarve armed with a repertoire of essential Portuguese phrases not only facilitates smoother communication but also earns you admiration and respect from the locals. Here are some indispensable phrases to add to your linguistic arsenal:

- Bom dia! - Good morning!
- Por favor - Please
- Obrigado/a - Thank you (masculine/feminine)
- De nada - You're welcome
- Onde fica...? - Where is...?
- Quanto custa? - How much does it cost?
- Desculpe - Excuse me/sorry
- Fala inglês? - Do you speak English?
- Uma mesa para dois, por favor - A table for two, please
- Adeus – Goodbye

Practice these phrases with enthusiasm and sincerity, and watch as doors of hospitality swing open before you, inviting you to partake in the rich tapestry of Algarvean life.

Cultural Insights:
Language serves as a gateway to understanding the cultural nuances and traditions of a destination. In the Algarve, where history whispers through ancient castles and echoes in the melodies of fado, grasping the subtleties of Portuguese communication deepens your appreciation for the region's heritage.

For instance, learning about the concept of "saudade," a uniquely Portuguese sentiment that encapsulates a melancholic longing for something or someone absent, enriches your understanding of the Algarvean soul. Through poetry, music, and heartfelt conversations, locals express this profound emotion, inviting you to share in their introspective journey.

Moreover, exploring the origins of Portuguese expressions and idioms adds layers of depth to your linguistic exploration. From the poetic imagery of "saudade" to the jovial banter of everyday conversations, each phrase carries with it a story, a history, and a connection to the soul of the Algarve.

Navigating Language Challenges:
While the Algarve embraces linguistic diversity and welcomes visitors from around the globe, navigating language challenges may arise, particularly in more remote or traditional areas. However, with patience, humility, and a willingness to learn, these obstacles transform into opportunities for growth and cultural exchange.

In instances where language barriers prove formidable, don't hesitate to utilize technology as a bridge to communication. Translation apps, phrasebooks, and language learning tools offer invaluable support, enabling you to navigate unfamiliar terrain with confidence and grace.

Furthermore, don't underestimate the power of non-verbal communication. A warm smile, a respectful gesture, or a genuine expression of gratitude transcends language barriers, forging connections that transcend words alone.

Safety Tips

While the region is renowned for its charm and hospitality, it's always wise to be prepared and informed to make the most of your travels. I'll share invaluable safety tips gleaned from years of local insight, ensuring your adventure in the Algarve is both exhilarating and secure.

Stay Aware of Your Surroundings:
The Algarve's stunning landscapes and bustling towns can captivate your attention, but it's crucial to remain vigilant and aware of your surroundings. Whether you're strolling through a charming village or lounging on a picturesque beach, keep an eye on your belongings and be mindful of any unfamiliar individuals or situations.

To get the most out of your experience, immerse yourself in the local culture while maintaining a level of awareness. Strike up conversations with friendly locals, savoring the flavors of authentic cuisine or discovering hidden gems off the beaten path. By staying present and observant, you'll enhance your journey while safeguarding your well-being.

Secure Your Valuables:
While the Algarve is generally safe for travelers, petty theft can occur, particularly in crowded tourist areas. To protect your belongings, invest in a secure travel wallet or pouch to store your passport, cash, and credit cards. Avoid carrying large sums of money or flashy jewelry that may attract unwanted attention.

When visiting popular attractions or lounging on the beach, never leave your belongings unattended. Utilize lockers or secure bags to store your valuables while exploring, ensuring peace of mind as you immerse yourself in the region's beauty. Additionally, consider using a discreet money belt or hidden pocket to safeguard your essentials while on the move.

Exercise Caution When Swimming:
The Algarve's pristine beaches and crystalline waters beckon travelers to indulge in refreshing swims and aquatic adventures. However, it's essential to exercise caution and adhere to safety guidelines to avoid potential risks, such as strong currents or undertows.

Before taking a dip, familiarize yourself with the beach's designated swimming areas and any warning signs indicating hazardous conditions. If you're unsure about the water's safety, consult with local lifeguards or beach attendants for guidance. Additionally, avoid swimming alone and always supervise children closely to prevent accidents.

To fully appreciate the Algarve's coastal splendor, consider embarking on a guided boat tour or snorkeling excursion led by experienced professionals. These guided adventures offer a safe and enriching way to explore the region's marine life and hidden treasures while ensuring your well-being.

Respect Local Customs and Laws:
As you immerse yourself in the Algarve's vibrant culture and traditions, it's essential to respect local customs and adhere to regional laws. Familiarize yourself with cultural etiquette, such as greeting locals with a friendly "Bom dia" (good morning) or "Boa tarde" (good afternoon), and dressing modestly when visiting religious sites or rural villages.

Additionally, be mindful of local regulations regarding alcohol consumption, public behavior, and environmental conservation. While indulging in Portugal's renowned wine or sampling regional delicacies, do so responsibly and in moderation, respecting the community and its values.

To gain deeper insights into the Algarve's rich heritage and customs, consider participating in cultural experiences such as cooking classes, traditional music performances, or guided walking tours. Engaging with local artisans and storytellers offers a meaningful way to connect with the region's history and traditions while fostering mutual respect and understanding.

Local Customs and Etiquette

The Algarvians, known for their warmth and hospitality, deeply value traditions and manners, and by understanding and respecting these customs, you'll not only enhance your travel experience but also forge meaningful connections with the locals.

Embracing Warmth and Hospitality

Algarvians are renowned for their genuine warmth and hospitality, and it's customary to greet others with a friendly "bom dia" (good morning), "boa tarde" (good afternoon), or "boa noite" (good evening), accompanied by a smile. Don't be surprised if locals engage you in conversation or offer assistance; they take pride in making visitors feel welcome.

Respect for Family and Community

Family plays a central role in Algarvian culture, and you'll often find multigenerational families gathering for meals or celebrations. If invited into a local's home, it's customary to remove your shoes at the door and express gratitude for their hospitality. Remember to greet elders with respect, addressing them as "senhor" (Mr.) or "senhora" (Mrs.), followed by their surname.

Appreciation for Leisurely Dining

Mealtime in the Algarve is a cherished affair, with an emphasis on savoring each dish and engaging in lively conversation. When dining out, it's common practice to wait for everyone to be served before beginning your meal and to keep your hands visible on the table. Refrain from discussing sensitive topics such as politics or religion, as these subjects are best avoided in polite company.

Honoring Traditions and Festivals

The Algarve boasts a calendar filled with vibrant festivals and cultural celebrations, each offering a glimpse into the region's rich heritage. Whether attending the annual Festa dos Tabuleiros in Tomar or the lively Carnival festivities in Loulé, embrace the opportunity to join in the merriment, sample traditional delicacies, and witness age-old customs come to life.

Respect for Nature and Environment

With its breathtaking coastline and pristine natural landscapes, the Algarve is a haven for eco-conscious travelers. Show respect for the environment by disposing of waste responsibly, using refillable water bottles, and supporting sustainable tourism initiatives. Take time to explore the region's protected areas, such as the Ria Formosa Natural Park, and learn about local conservation efforts.

Navigating Social Interactions

In social settings, Algarvians value direct communication and honesty, so don't be afraid to express your opinions or engage in spirited discussions. However, it's important to maintain a level of politeness and avoid raising your voice or interrupting others. If invited to someone's home, consider bringing a small gift, such as flowers or pastries, as a token of appreciation.

Understanding Time and Punctuality

While the pace of life in the Algarve may seem relaxed, punctuality is still highly regarded, especially for business meetings or formal events. Arrive on time or slightly early to show respect for others' schedules and commitments. If running late, it's courteous to call and inform your host or colleagues.

Dressing Appropriately

The Algarve enjoys a Mediterranean climate, with mild winters and hot summers, so dress accordingly for the season.

In beach towns, casual attire such as shorts, sundresses, and sandals is acceptable, but when visiting churches or upscale restaurants, opt for more modest clothing out of respect for local customs. Additionally, remember to cover up before entering religious sites.

Navigating Social Hierarchies

While the Algarvian society is egalitarian, there is still a degree of respect for social hierarchies, particularly in formal settings. Addressing individuals with their appropriate titles, such as "Doutor" (Doctor) or "Engenheiro" (Engineer), acknowledges their professional accomplishments and status. When in doubt, err on the side of formality until invited to use a more familiar tone.

Gratitude and Farewells

As your time in the Algarve draws to a close, express gratitude to those who have enriched your experience with their kindness and hospitality. A heartfelt "obrigado" (thank you) accompanied by a warm handshake or embrace is a simple yet meaningful way to show appreciation. Until we meet again, bid farewell with a sincere "adeus" (goodbye) and the hope of returning one day.

Resources

Transportation Guide

Picture yourself standing on the golden sands of Praia da Marinha, the Atlantic breeze tousling your hair as the sun dips below the horizon, casting hues of pink and orange across the sky. To truly immerse yourself in this coastal paradise, you'll need to know how to navigate its winding roads and charming villages. Fear not, for this transportation guide will be your compass, guiding you through the myriad of options to ensure your journey through the Algarve is seamless and unforgettable.

Getting There:

- Whether you're arriving by air, land, or sea, reaching the Algarve is easier than you think. The region is served by Faro International Airport, conveniently located just a short drive from the main tourist hubs. From the airport, you can opt for a hassle-free transfer via taxi, shuttle bus, or private car hire to your accommodation.

- For those traveling by train, Portugal's extensive railway network connects major cities like Lisbon and Porto to Faro, offering scenic views of the countryside along the way. Once you arrive in Faro, local trains and buses provide convenient links to destinations across the Algarve.

- If you prefer the freedom of the open road, renting a car allows you to explore the Algarve at your own pace. Major car rental companies operate at Faro Airport, offering a wide range of vehicles to suit your needs. From sleek convertibles to spacious SUVs, you'll find the perfect ride to embark on your Algarve adventure.

- Traveling by sea is also an option, with ferry services connecting the Algarve to neighboring destinations like Spain and Morocco. Whether you arrive by plane, train, car, or boat, the journey to the Algarve promises to be as enchanting as the destination itself.

Getting Around:

- Once you've arrived in the Algarve, getting around is a breeze thanks to the region's efficient transportation network. Local buses operate regular routes between towns and villages, making it easy to explore nearby attractions without the hassle of driving.

- For a more scenic mode of transport, why not hop aboard a vintage tram or quaint tuk-tuk? These charming vehicles offer guided tours of popular destinations like Lagos and Albufeira, giving you a unique perspective on the Algarve's rich history and culture.

- Cycling enthusiasts will delight in the Algarve's extensive network of bike paths and scenic coastal routes. Renting a bike allows you to soak up the sun while pedaling your way from one picturesque village to the next, stopping to sample local delicacies along the way.

- If you're pressed for time or simply prefer the convenience of door-to-door service, taxis and ride-sharing apps are readily available throughout the Algarve. Whether you're heading to the beach, a restaurant, or a hidden gem off the beaten path, a quick call or tap of the app is all it takes to summon a ride.

- For those craving a taste of adventure, why not explore the Algarve's waterways by kayak or stand-up paddleboard? Guided tours offer the chance to paddle through sea caves, explore secluded beaches, and spot marine life beneath the crystal-clear waters of the Atlantic Ocean.

Recommended Websites and Apps

As you prepare to embark on your journey to the enchanting Algarve, it's essential to arm yourself with the right tools to make the most of your adventure. In today's digital age, a plethora of websites and apps can serve as your trusty companions, offering invaluable insights, real-time updates, and insider tips to ensure a seamless and unforgettable experience. Let's delve into some of the top recommended resources tailored to enhance your exploration of this coastal paradise.

Algarve Tourism Board Website (www.visitalgarve.pt)
Your first port of call should undoubtedly be the official website of the Algarve Tourism Board. Here, you'll find a treasure trove of information curated by local experts, offering comprehensive guides on everything from must-visit attractions to lesser-known hidden gems tucked away in the region's charming corners. Dive into detailed itineraries, browse through captivating photo galleries, and uncover insightful articles penned by seasoned travelers and passionate locals alike. Whether you're seeking inspiration for your next adventure or practical advice on logistics and accommodations, this website serves as your ultimate gateway to unlocking the wonders of the Algarve.

Visit Algarve App
For travelers on the go, the Visit Algarve app is a convenient companion designed to enhance your exploration in real-time. Available for both iOS and Android devices, this user-friendly app puts the entire region at your fingertips, offering

interactive maps, up-to-date event listings, and personalized recommendations based on your preferences and location. Navigate with ease as you discover nearby attractions, dining hotspots, and hidden treasures off the beaten path. With integrated features such as offline access and language support, the Visit Algarve app ensures that your journey is seamless, stress-free, and tailored to your individual interests.

TripAdvisor (www.tripadvisor.com)
When it comes to crowd-sourced wisdom and peer-reviewed recommendations, TripAdvisor reigns supreme as the go-to platform for discerning travelers worldwide. Harnessing the collective insights of millions of users, this dynamic website and app provide an extensive database of reviews, ratings, and insider tips for every aspect of your Algarve adventure. Whether you're scouting for top-rated restaurants, seeking guidance on accommodations, or craving off-the-beaten-path experiences, TripAdvisor offers invaluable guidance to help you make informed decisions and uncover hidden gems that may have eluded even the most seasoned explorers.

Airbnb (www.airbnb.com)
For those craving a more personalized and immersive travel experience, Airbnb offers a diverse array of accommodations ranging from cozy apartments and boutique guesthouses to luxurious villas and off-grid retreats. Skip the cookie-cutter hotels and embrace the charm of local living as you browse through an extensive selection of unique listings curated by Algarve's hospitable hosts. Immerse yourself in the region's vibrant culture, savoring authentic cuisine, and forging meaningful connections with your hosts and fellow travelers. With Airbnb's intuitive platform and secure booking process, you can embark on a tailor-made journey that resonates with your individual style and preferences.

Google Maps

No exploration of the Algarve would be complete without the indispensable guidance of Google Maps. Seamlessly navigate winding coastal roads, picturesque villages, and hidden trails with confidence, thanks to this ubiquitous mapping service. Whether you're embarking on a scenic road trip along the rugged coastline or seeking out hidden beaches nestled among dramatic cliffs, Google Maps offers real-time navigation, traffic updates, and offline access to ensure that you never lose your way. From bustling city centers to remote countryside retreats, let Google Maps be your trusted companion as you embark on your Algarve adventure with ease and peace of mind.

Instagram

In today's visually driven world, Instagram serves as more than just a social media platform – it's a window into the soul of the Algarve, showcasing its breathtaking beauty and vibrant culture through the lenses of passionate travelers and local photographers. Follow hashtags such as #Algarve or #VisitAlgarve to discover a curated feed of stunning images capturing the region's golden beaches, turquoise waters, and picturesque sunsets. From hidden coves accessible only by boat to charming cobblestone streets lined with colorful houses, let Instagram inspire your wanderlust and guide you towards unforgettable experiences that await in every corner of the Algarve.

WhatsApp

As you immerse yourself in the warmth and hospitality of the Algarve, staying connected with friends, family, and fellow travelers is essential for sharing precious moments and coordinating plans. Enter WhatsApp – the ubiquitous messaging app that transcends borders and bridges distances with its seamless communication features. Create group chats with your travel companions, exchange tips and recommendations with fellow explorers, and stay in touch with local guides and hosts for insider insights and last-minute updates. Whether you're arranging a sunset boat tour or coordinating a beachside picnic, WhatsApp keeps you connected and in sync throughout your Algarve adventure.

Algarve Daily News (www.algarvedailynews.com)
For those craving a deeper understanding of the local culture, politics, and current events shaping life in the Algarve, the Algarve Daily News offers a unique window into the region's pulse. As the leading English-language news source serving the Algarve community, this online publication provides a diverse range of articles, features, and opinion pieces covering everything from lifestyle and travel to business and environmental issues. Stay informed about upcoming events, cultural festivals, and community initiatives that enrich your experience and foster a deeper connection with the people and places of the Algarve.

Conclusion

Final Tips and Recommendations

As your journey through the enchanting Algarve draws to a close, allow me to impart some final pearls of wisdom to ensure your experience lingers in your memories like the warm embrace of the Mediterranean sun.

First and foremost, let's talk about time. The Algarve is a land where time seems to slow down, where the gentle rhythm of the waves and the whispering breeze through the almond trees beckon you to savor each moment. So, my dear traveler, resist the urge to rush through your days here. Embrace the concept of "saudade," a uniquely Portuguese feeling of longing and nostalgia, and allow yourself to truly immerse in the beauty that surrounds you.

Now, onto practical matters. As you prepare to bid adieu to this slice of paradise, it's essential to tie up any loose ends regarding your accommodation, transportation, and belongings. Double-check your departure arrangements, whether it's confirming your flight or ensuring your rental car is returned on time. Take a moment to reflect on the memories you've made and the experiences you've cherished during your stay.

Before you leave, indulge in one last culinary delight. Whether it's a succulent seafood feast at a seaside taverna, a steaming bowl of freshly caught cataplana, or a sweet pastel de nata enjoyed with a strong espresso, let your taste buds savor the flavors of the Algarve one final time. And don't forget to pick up some souvenirs to take home—a bottle of local wine, a jar of tangy piri-piri sauce, or a hand-painted ceramic tile—to remind you of your time in this magical corner of the world.

As you prepare to depart, take a moment to reflect on the beauty you've encountered during your journey. Whether it's the breathtaking vistas of the rugged coastline, the warmth of the Algarvian hospitality, or the vibrant colors of the local markets, let these memories be your souvenirs, cherished keepsakes that will accompany you long after you've returned home.

But perhaps the most important recommendation I can offer is this: keep the spirit of the Algarve alive within you. Let the sense of serenity and tranquility you've discovered here guide you in your daily life. Whether it's taking a moment to watch the sunset, savoring a leisurely meal with loved ones, or simply finding joy in the simple pleasures of each day, carry the essence of the Algarve with you wherever you go.

And so, my dear traveler, as you bid farewell to the Algarve, remember that though your time here may be fleeting, the memories you've created will last a lifetime. Until we meet again, may your journeys be filled with adventure, discovery, and the boundless beauty of the world around you. Safe travels, and may the spirit of the Algarve be with you always.

Share Your Experience

it's time to reflect on your journey through the captivating realm of Algarve. Sharing your experience isn't just about recounting your adventures; it's about connecting with others, inspiring future travelers, and preserving the memories that have woven themselves into the fabric of your soul during your time in this enchanting region.

Connect with Fellow Travelers: One of the most enriching aspects of travel is the opportunity to connect with people from all walks of life, each with their own tales to tell. Whether you're swapping stories over a glass of vinho verde in a cozy tavern or striking up a conversation with a fellow hiker along the rugged cliffs, take the time to engage with those around you. You never know what fascinating insights or unexpected friendships may blossom from these chance encounters.

Capture the Moment: In the age of smartphones and social media, it's easier than ever to document your travels with a simple click of a button. But don't let the pursuit of the perfect Instagram shot overshadow the raw beauty of the moment. Take the time to savor the sights, sounds, and sensations that surround you, allowing them to seep into your consciousness and etch themselves into your memory. Then, when the time is right, snap a photo or two to serve as a memento of your experiences.

Write a Travel Journal: There's something inherently magical about putting pen to paper and chronicling your adventures in a travel journal. Whether you prefer to jot down your thoughts in a leather-bound notebook or compose eloquent prose on your laptop beneath the shade of an ancient olive tree, keeping a record of your journey allows you to capture the nuances and emotions that photographs alone cannot convey. Let your words flow freely as you recount the highs and lows, the moments of triumph and vulnerability that have shaped your time in Algarve.

Share Your Insights Online: In today's digital age, the internet serves as a vast repository of travel tips, reviews, and personal anecdotes. Consider sharing your experiences on travel forums, blogs, or social media platforms, where your insights can help fellow adventurers navigate the intricacies of planning their own Algarve escapades. Whether you're raving about a hidden gem of a restaurant tucked away in a sleepy village or offering sage advice on avoiding tourist traps, your contributions have the power to make a difference in the lives of others.

Preserve Your Memories: Long after the sun has set on your Algarve adventure and you've returned to the rhythm of everyday life, your memories will serve as cherished souvenirs of your time spent in this idyllic corner of the world. Whether it's a seashell plucked from the shores of a secluded beach, a handcrafted ceramic tile purchased from a local artisan, or a snippet of conversation shared with a kindred spirit, hold onto these tangible reminders of the magic you've experienced. They are the threads that bind you to the tapestry of Algarve, weaving a story that is uniquely yours to share.

In the end, sharing your experience is about more than just recounting the places you've been or the things you've seen. It's about forging connections, preserving memories, and embracing the transformative power of travel. So as you bid farewell to Algarve and carry its spirit with you wherever your journey may lead, remember to share the magic with those around you, for in doing so, you breathe new life into the timeless allure of this captivating region.

Farewell to Algarve

As your journey in the Algarve draws to a close, it's time to bid farewell to this enchanting region. But before you depart, let's take a moment to reflect on the memories you've made and the experiences you've had during your stay.

As the sun sets over the horizon, casting a golden glow over the coastline, you might find yourself feeling a twinge of sadness at leaving behind such beauty. But fear not, for the memories you've created here will stay with you forever, serving as a reminder of the magic of the Algarve.

As you prepare to say goodbye, take some time to savor the last moments of your trip. Perhaps you'll wander down to the beach one final time, feeling the soft sand between your toes and listening to the gentle lapping of the waves. Or maybe you'll find a quiet spot to sit and watch the sunset, marveling at the kaleidoscope of colors painting the sky.

But the farewell is not just about saying goodbye to the natural beauty of the Algarve – it's also about bidding farewell to the people you've met along the way. From the friendly locals who welcomed you with open arms to the fellow travelers who shared their stories and adventures, the connections you've made here have added depth and richness to your experience.

As you reflect on your time in the Algarve, take a moment to appreciate the cultural richness of the region. Whether you've explored historic sites like the Castle of Silves or immersed yourself in the vibrant atmosphere of local markets and festivals, the Algarve has offered you a glimpse into its rich heritage and traditions.

But perhaps the most important part of saying farewell to the Algarve is expressing gratitude for the experiences you've had and the memories you've made. Take a moment to thank the universe for the opportunity to explore this beautiful corner of the world and to cherish the moments you've shared with loved ones.

As you pack your bags and prepare to leave, know that the Algarve will always hold a special place in your heart. Whether you return again someday or carry the memories with you wherever you go, the beauty and magic of this region will continue to inspire and uplift you.

And so, as you bid farewell to the Algarve, remember to take one last deep breath of the salty sea air, feel the warmth of the sun on your skin, and carry the spirit of this place with you as you journey onward. Until we meet again, may your travels be filled with adventure, joy, and the enduring beauty of the Algarve.

BONUS SECTION

Itinerary Suggestions

Outdoor Adventure Itinerary

Day 1: Surf, Sand, and Sea

Morning: Start your day with an adrenaline-packed adventure by heading to Praia da Marinha, one of the most stunning beaches in Algarve. Located near Lagoa, this beach boasts breathtaking cliffs, crystal-clear waters, and golden sands. As you arrive, you'll be greeted by the sight of jagged rock formations rising majestically from the sea.

Activities: Embark on a kayak tour to explore the hidden caves and grottoes along the coastline. Several local tour companies offer guided kayak excursions, providing you with the opportunity to paddle through sea arches and marvel at the geological wonders of the region. Alternatively, if you're an experienced surfer or eager to learn, join a surf lesson and catch some waves at nearby surf spots such as Praia do Amado or Praia da Arrifana.

Cost: A guided kayak tour typically ranges from $30 to $50 per person, including equipment rental and instruction. Surf lessons start at around $40 for a group session.

Lunch: After working up an appetite, treat yourself to a delicious seafood lunch at O Sargo Restaurant. Nestled in the charming village of Carvoeiro, this restaurant specializes in fresh fish and seafood dishes prepared with locally sourced ingredients. Indulge in grilled sardines, seafood rice, or the renowned cataplana—a traditional Portuguese seafood stew.

- Address: O Sargo Restaurant, Rua do Barranco 20, 8400-527 Carvoeiro, Portugal
- Phone: +351 282 357 145
- Opening Hours: 12:00 PM - 3:00 PM, 7:00 PM - 10:00 PM (Closed on Mondays)
- Website: www.osargo.com

Afternoon: After lunch, continue your outdoor adventure by exploring the dramatic cliffs and hidden beaches of Ponta da Piedade. Located near Lagos, this natural wonder offers spectacular panoramic views of the Atlantic Ocean. Take a leisurely stroll along the cliff-top pathways or descend the staircase to reach the secluded coves and grottoes below.

Activities: Opt for a boat tour to fully appreciate the beauty of Ponta da Piedade from the water. Boat tours depart regularly from Lagos Marina and take you on a scenic journey along the coastline, allowing you to admire the towering rock formations and turquoise waters up close.

Cost: Boat tours typically range from $15 to $30 per person for a 1-hour excursion.

Evening: As the sun begins to set, head back to Lagos and unwind with a refreshing drink at one of the beachfront bars along Meia Praia. Watch as the sky transforms into a palette of vibrant hues, casting a golden glow over the landscape. For dinner, savor the flavors of traditional Portuguese cuisine at Tasca do Kiko, a cozy restaurant renowned for its grilled fish and seafood specialties.

- Address: Tasca do Kiko, Rua António Barbosa Viana, 8600-593 Lagos, Portugal
- Phone: +351 282 799 095
- Opening Hours: 7:00 PM - 10:30 PM (Closed on Sundays)

Day 2: Exploring Nature's Playground

Morning: Rise early and embark on a hiking adventure in the Ria Formosa Natural Park. Stretching along the eastern coast of Algarve, this protected area is a haven for wildlife and boasts diverse ecosystems, including salt marshes, lagoons, and barrier islands. Start your exploration at the Quinta do Lago Nature Reserve, where you can follow scenic trails surrounded by pine forests and wetlands.

Activities: Keep an eye out for native bird species such as flamingos, spoonbills, and purple herons as you hike through the park. Birdwatching enthusiasts can also visit the nearby Ludo and Salgados Lagoon, which serve as important feeding and nesting grounds for migratory birds.

Cost: Entrance to the Quinta do Lago Nature Reserve is typically free of charge. Guided birdwatching tours may be available for an additional fee.

Lunch: After working up an appetite, head to Restaurante A Venda, a hidden gem tucked away in the village of Estói. This family-run restaurant offers a warm and inviting atmosphere, along with delicious regional dishes made from fresh, locally sourced ingredients. Treat yourself to a hearty meal of grilled octopus, seafood cataplana, or Algarvian-style chicken.

- **Address**: Restaurante A Venda, Estrada Nacional 2, 8005-465 Estói, Portugal
- **Phone**: +351 289 998 680
- **Opening Hours: 12:00 PM - 3:00 PM, 7:00 PM - 10:00 PM** (Closed on Tuesdays)

Afternoon: Spend the afternoon exploring the rugged beauty of the Costa Vicentina Natural Park, located along the western coast of Algarve. This unspoiled wilderness is characterized by towering cliffs, pristine beaches, and rolling hills dotted with wildflowers. Head to Praia do Amado, a renowned surfing spot, and marvel at the power of the Atlantic Ocean as you watch surfers ride the waves.

Activities: If you're feeling adventurous, embark on a horseback riding excursion along the coastal trails of Costa Vicentina. Several local stables offer guided horseback riding tours, allowing you to discover hidden coves and scenic viewpoints while enjoying the freedom of riding on horseback.

Cost: Horseback riding tours typically range from $50 to $100 per person for a 2-hour ride.

Evening: Return to your accommodation and relax after a day of outdoor exploration. For dinner, venture into the historic town of Aljezur and dine at Restaurante O Paulo. This charming eatery specializes in traditional Algarvian cuisine, with a focus on fresh seafood and hearty stews. Be sure to try the grilled fish of the day or the signature cataplana de marisco for a truly authentic dining experience.

- Address: Restaurante O Paulo, Rua 25 de Abril 74, 8670-088 Aljezur, Portugal
- Phone: +351 282 998 234
- Opening Hours: 7:00 PM - 10:30 PM (Closed on Wednesdays)

Day 3: Conquering the Great Outdoors

Morning: Begin your day with an exhilarating adventure at Serra de Monchique, the highest mountain range in Algarve. Lace up your hiking boots and explore the network of trails that wind through lush forests, cascading waterfalls, and panoramic viewpoints. Start your ascent from the picturesque village of Monchique and make your way to the summit of Foia, where you'll be rewarded with sweeping views of the surrounding countryside and coastline.

Activities: For a unique experience, consider joining a guided jeep safari tour that takes you off the beaten path and deep into the heart of Serra de Monchique. Traverse rugged terrain, discover hidden valleys, and learn about the region's flora and fauna from knowledgeable local guides.

Cost: Jeep safari tours typically range from $50 to $80 per person for a half-day excursion.

Lunch: After working up an appetite, head to the charming town of Monchique and enjoy a leisurely lunch at Chorilongo. This rustic restaurant specializes in traditional Algarvian cuisine, with a focus on hearty grilled meats, savory stews, and homemade desserts. Savor the flavors of slow-cooked lamb, grilled chorizo, or the famous feijoada—a hearty bean stew.

- Address: Chorilongo, Rua do Poço Novo 7, 8550-405 Monchique, Portugal
- Phone: +351 282 911 587
- Opening Hours: 12:00 PM - 3:00 PM, 7:00 PM - 10:00 PM (Closed on Mondays)

Afternoon: After lunch, immerse yourself in the natural beauty of the Algarve countryside with a visit to Rocha da Pena. This stunning limestone ridge is located near Loulé and offers a network of hiking trails that meander through pine forests, rocky outcrops, and scenic viewpoints. Take your time to explore the diverse landscapes and keep an eye out for native wildlife such as eagles, wild boar, and hoopoes.

Activities: For a memorable experience, embark on a rock climbing adventure and test your skills on the rugged cliffs of

Rocha da Pena. Several local outdoor adventure companies offer guided rock climbing excursions suitable for climbers of all levels, providing you with the opportunity to challenge yourself while enjoying panoramic views of the surrounding countryside.

Cost: Rock climbing tours typically range from $50 to $100 per person for a half-day session, including equipment rental and instruction.

Evening: As the day draws to a close, head back to your accommodation and unwind after a day of outdoor exploration. For a memorable dining experience, venture into the historic town of Loulé and dine at Avenida 5 de Outubro. This elegant restaurant offers a sophisticated ambiance and a diverse menu featuring innovative interpretations of traditional Portuguese dishes. Indulge in seafood risotto, grilled steak, or the chef's tasting menu for a culinary journey through the flavors of Algarve.

- Address: Avenida 5 de Outubro, 8100-270 Loulé, Portugal
- Phone: +351 289 414 421
- Opening Hours: 12:00 PM - 3:00 PM, 7:00 PM - 10:00 PM (Closed on Sundays)

Romantic itinerary

Day 1: Exploring Quaint Villages and Sunset Dinners

Morning:
Begin your romantic journey through the Algarve by immersing yourselves in the charm of its quaint villages. Head to the picturesque town of Alte, nestled amidst rolling hills and lush greenery. Wander through its cobblestone streets adorned with colorful flowers, and don't miss a visit to the

Fonte Pequena, a natural spring where you can fill your bottles with fresh water believed to have healing properties.

- Cost: Free

- Address: Alte, Loulé, Portugal

Afternoon:
Continue your journey to the enchanting village of Monchique, located in the scenic Serra de Monchique mountains. Explore its narrow streets lined with whitewashed houses and artisan shops. Make sure to visit the Miradouro da Picota viewpoint for breathtaking panoramic views of the surrounding landscape.

- Cost: Free

- Address: Monchique, Portugal

Evening:
As the sun begins to set, head to the coastal town of Carvoeiro for a romantic dinner overlooking the ocean. Indulge in fresh seafood dishes at Restaurante O Pescador, known for its intimate ambiance and stunning views of the cliffs and sea.

- Cost: Approximately $50-$100 per person

- Address: Restaurante O Pescador, Praia do Carvoeiro, 8400-517 Carvoeiro, Portugal

- Contact: +351 282 357 663

Day 2: Beach Picnics and Sunset Cruises

Morning:
Start your day with a leisurely breakfast at your accommodation, savoring local pastries and freshly brewed coffee. Then, pack a picnic basket with your favorite treats and head to Praia da Marinha, one of the most beautiful beaches in the Algarve. Find a secluded spot on the golden sands and enjoy a romantic picnic while listening to the sound of the waves crashing against the cliffs.

- Cost: $20-$50 for picnic supplies

- Address: Praia da Marinha, Lagoa, Portugal

Afternoon:
In the afternoon, embark on a sunset cruise along the Algarve coastline. Feel the gentle sea breeze on your skin as you sail past towering cliffs, hidden caves, and secluded beaches. Many tour operators offer sunset cruises departing from Albufeira or Lagos, with options for private charters or group excursions.

- Cost: $50-$100 per person

- Address: Marina de Albufeira, 8200-394 Albufeira, Portugal

- Contact: +351 289 598 023

Evening:
After the cruise, treat yourselves to a romantic dinner at Vila Joya, a Michelin-starred restaurant located in a luxurious boutique hotel overlooking the ocean. Indulge in a gourmet tasting menu paired with fine wines, and savor every moment of this unforgettable dining experience.

- Cost: Approximately $200-$300 per person for tasting menu with wine pairing

- Address: Vila Joya, Estrada da Galé, Albufeira, Portugal

- Contact: +351 289 591 795

Day 3: Spa Retreat and Sunset Strolls

Morning:
Relax and rejuvenate together with a couples' spa treatment at one of the Algarve's renowned wellness retreats. Pamper yourselves with massages, facials, and other therapeutic treatments amidst tranquil surroundings. Whether you choose a spa located in the countryside or by the coast, you're sure to leave feeling refreshed and revitalized.

- Cost: $100-$300 per person for spa treatments

- Address: The Monchique Resort & Spa, Lugar do Montinho, 8550-232 Monchique, Portugal

- Contact: +351 282 240 130

Afternoon:
Take a leisurely stroll along the cliffs of Ponta da Piedade, hand in hand with your loved one, as you admire the breathtaking views of the Atlantic Ocean and the rugged coastline. Marvel at the intricate rock formations and hidden grottoes carved by the sea over centuries, and don't forget to capture the magical moments with your camera.

- Cost: Free

- Address: Ponta da Piedade, 8600-544 Lagos, Portugal

Evening:
As the day draws to a close, enjoy a romantic sunset dinner at Casa do Campo, a charming restaurant nestled in the countryside near Albufeira. Feast on traditional Portuguese dishes made with locally sourced ingredients, and toast to your unforgettable romantic getaway in the Algarve.

- Cost: Approximately $50-$100 per person

- Address: Casa do Campo, Estrada Vale de Parra, Albufeira, Portugal

- Contact: +351 289 588 393

Coastal itinerary

Day 1: Beach Hopping and Seafood Feasts

Morning:
Start your coastal adventure by exploring some of the Algarve's most iconic beaches. Begin with Praia da Falésia, renowned for its stunning red cliffs and golden sands stretching for miles along the coastline. Take a leisurely stroll along the beach, dip your toes in the crystal-clear waters, and soak up the sun on the soft sand.

- Cost: Free

- Address: Praia da Falésia, Albufeira, Portugal

Afternoon:
For lunch, indulge in a feast of fresh seafood at Restaurante Praia Dourada, a charming beachfront restaurant located on Praia da Oura. Savor grilled fish, seafood paella, and other delicious dishes while enjoying panoramic views of the ocean.

Don't forget to try the local specialty, cataplana, a flavorful seafood stew cooked in a traditional copper pot.

- Cost: Approximately $30-$50 per person

- Address: Restaurante Praia Dourada, Praia da Oura, 8200-269 Albufeira, Portugal

- Contact: +351 289 589 036

Evening:
As the sun begins to set, head to the bustling town of Albufeira for an evening of entertainment and nightlife. Explore the narrow streets of the Old Town, lined with lively bars, restaurants, and shops. Grab a cocktail at one of the beachfront bars and enjoy live music or a DJ set as you soak up the vibrant atmosphere.

- Cost: Varies depending on drinks and entertainment

- Address: Albufeira Old Town, Albufeira, Portugal

Day 2: Coastal Adventures and Cliff Exploration

Morning:
Embark on an adventurous kayaking tour along the Algarve coast, exploring hidden caves, grottoes, and secluded beaches inaccessible by land. Many tour operators offer guided kayak excursions departing from Lagos or Albufeira, providing all necessary equipment and expert instruction for a safe and memorable experience on the water.

- Cost: $40-$80 per person

- Address: Kayak tours depart from various locations in Lagos and Albufeira

- Contact: Algarve Kayak Tours - www.algarvekayaktours.com

Afternoon:
After your kayaking adventure, continue your exploration of the Algarve's stunning coastline by visiting Ponta da Piedade. Take a boat tour or rent a kayak to venture into the intricate network of sea caves and rock formations sculpted by the sea. Marvel at the towering cliffs, arches, and tunnels, and don't forget to capture the breathtaking scenery with your camera.

- Cost: Boat tours: $20-$40 per person, Kayak rental: $30-$50 per person

- Address: Ponta da Piedade, 8600-544 Lagos, Portugal

Evening:
For dinner, head to Restaurante A Ruína, located in a restored 17th-century fortress overlooking the sea in the charming town of Carvoeiro. Indulge in Mediterranean-inspired cuisine made with locally sourced ingredients, accompanied by fine wines and panoramic views of the coastline illuminated by the setting sun.

- Cost: Approximately $40-$80 per person

- Address: Restaurante A Ruína, Fortaleza de Nossa Senhora da Encarnação, Praia do Carvoeiro, 8400-525 Carvoeiro, Portugal

- Contact: +351 282 358 317

Day 3: Coastal Trails and Sunset Cocktails

Morning:
Start your day with a scenic hike along the Seven Hanging Valleys Trail, considered one of the most beautiful coastal walks in the Algarve. This cliff-top trail stretches from Praia da Marinha to Praia de Vale Centeanes, offering breathtaking views of the Atlantic Ocean, dramatic cliffs, and hidden beaches along the way.

- Cost: Free

- Address: Seven Hanging Valleys Trail, Lagoa, Portugal

Afternoon:
After your hike, reward yourselves with a relaxing afternoon at Praia do Camilo, a secluded beach nestled between towering cliffs near Lagos. Spend your time swimming in the turquoise waters, sunbathing on the golden sands, or exploring the sea caves and rock formations along the coastline.

- Cost: Free

- Address: Praia do Camilo, Lagos, Portugal

Evening:
As the day comes to a close, head to the rooftop bar of Tivoli Carvoeiro for sunset cocktails with panoramic views of the ocean. Sip on creative cocktails crafted by expert mixologists, while enjoying the vibrant colors of the sunset painting the sky over the Algarve coast.

- Cost: Approximately $10-$20 per cocktail

- Address: Sky Bar, Tivoli Carvoeiro, Rua Anneliese Pohl, 8400-450 Carvoeiro, Portugal

- Contact: +351 282 351 100

Budget friendly itinerary

Day 1: Exploring the Coastal Beauty

Welcome to the Algarve, where every corner holds a piece of paradise waiting to be discovered. If you're traveling on a budget, fear not, for this itinerary will guide you through the wonders of this region without breaking the bank. Let's embark on a journey of coastal exploration and cultural immersion.

Morning: Praia da Marinha

Our adventure begins at Praia da Marinha, one of the most breathtaking beaches in the Algarve. Located near the town of Lagoa, this picturesque spot boasts golden sands, crystal-clear waters, and iconic limestone cliffs sculpted by the sea over centuries. Spend the morning soaking up the sun, taking refreshing dips in the ocean, or simply admiring the stunning vistas.

- Average Cost: Free

- Opening Hours: Open all day

- Directions: Praia da Marinha, Lagoa, Algarve, Portugal

- Amenities: Parking available, restroom facilities nearby

Afternoon: Explore Historic Silves

After a morning of seaside bliss, head inland to the historic town of Silves, known for its Moorish castle and charming cobblestone streets. Wander through the town's quaint squares, visit the impressive Silves Cathedral, and climb to the top of the castle for panoramic views of the surrounding countryside. Don't miss the opportunity to sample traditional Portuguese cuisine at one of the local eateries, where hearty meals come at affordable prices.

- Average Cost: Castle admission - $5/£4, meals - $10-$15/£8-£12 per person

- Opening Hours: Castle - 9:00 AM to 5:30 PM (closed on Mondays)

- Address: Castelo de Silves, Rua do Castelo, 8300-144 Silves, Portugal

- Contact: +351 282 440 800

- Amenities: Restrooms, guided tours available

Evening: Sunset at Praia da Rocha

As the day draws to a close, make your way to Praia da Rocha, one of the Algarve's liveliest beaches, famed for its vibrant atmosphere and stunning sunsets. Join locals and fellow travelers alike as you watch the sun dip below the horizon, casting a golden glow over the cliffs and sea. Afterward, explore the beachfront promenade lined with restaurants, bars, and souvenir shops, where you can enjoy a budget-friendly meal or sip on refreshing cocktails.

- Average Cost: Free (dining and drinks prices vary)

- Opening Hours: Open all day
- Directions: Praia da Rocha, Portimão, Algarve, Portugal
- Amenities: Beachfront restaurants, bars, shops

Day 2: Nature and Adventure

Embrace the natural beauty and outdoor adventures that the Algarve has to offer on the second day of your budget-friendly itinerary.

Morning: Hiking in Monchique

Escape the crowds and immerse yourself in the tranquil landscapes of the Serra de Monchique, a mountain range located in the western Algarve. Lace up your hiking boots and follow the trails that wind through lush forests, past cascading waterfalls, and alongside streams. Keep an eye out for native wildlife and enjoy the peaceful serenity of nature.

- Average Cost: Free (some guided tours available at additional cost)
- Opening Hours: Trails open all day
- Directions: Serra de Monchique, Monchique, Algarve, Portugal
- Amenities: Parking available at trailheads, restroom facilities at some locations

Afternoon: Beach Picnic at Praia de Benagil

After a morning of exploration, head to Praia de Benagil, a picturesque beach nestled beneath towering cliffs and famous for its stunning sea cave, the Benagil Cave. Bring along a picnic lunch of local delicacies, such as freshly baked bread, cured meats, and artisanal cheeses, and enjoy a leisurely afternoon soaking up the sun and swimming in the turquoise waters.

- Average Cost: Free (cost of picnic supplies varies)

- Opening Hours: Open all day

- Directions: Praia de Benagil, Lagoa, Algarve, Portugal

- Amenities: Limited facilities, beach access by boat or steep staircase

Evening: Stargazing at Sagres

End your day with a celestial spectacle at Cape St. Vincent, near the town of Sagres, known as "the end of the world" in ancient times. Settle in on the rugged cliffs overlooking the Atlantic Ocean and marvel at the vast expanse of stars twinkling overhead. With minimal light pollution, this remote location offers unparalleled opportunities for stargazing and contemplating the universe.

- Average Cost: Free

- Opening Hours: Open all day (best for stargazing after sunset)

- Directions: Cape St. Vincent, Sagres, Algarve, Portugal

- Amenities: Limited facilities, dress warmly and bring a blanket or chair

Day 3: Cultural Immersion

On the final day of your budget-friendly itinerary, delve into the rich culture and heritage of the Algarve.

Morning: Local Market in Loulé

Start your day with a visit to the bustling market in the town of Loulé, where vendors sell everything from fresh produce and regional specialties to handmade crafts and souvenirs. Immerse yourself in the vibrant atmosphere, haggle for bargains, and interact with locals as you sample delicious treats like olives, cheeses, and pastries.

- Average Cost: Free (cost of purchases varies)
- Opening Hours: Market - 7:00 AM to 3:00 PM (closed on Sundays)
- Address: Mercado Municipal de Loulé, Largo do Mercado, 8100-280 Loulé, Portugal
- Contact: +351 289 400 829
- Amenities: Restrooms, parking nearby

Afternoon: Cultural Tour of Faro

In the afternoon, explore the charming city of Faro, the capital of the Algarve region, and discover its rich history and cultural landmarks. Take a leisurely stroll through the historic old town, where narrow alleys lead to picturesque squares, traditional whitewashed buildings, and historic monuments such as the Faro Cathedral and the Arco da Vila. Don't forget to wander through the Jardim Manuel Bivar, a beautiful garden overlooking the marina.

- Average Cost: Free (guided tours available at additional cost)

- Opening Hours: Faro Cathedral - 9:30 AM to 5:30 PM (closed on Sundays), Jardim Manuel Bivar - Open all day

- Address: Faro Cathedral, Largo da Sé, 8000-138 Faro, Portugal; Jardim Manuel Bivar, Avenida da República, 8000-076 Faro, Portugal

- Contact: Faro Cathedral - +351 289 806 898

- Amenities: Restrooms, guided tours available

Evening: Fado Performance in Albufeira

Conclude your budget-friendly journey with an evening of traditional Portuguese music at a Fado house in Albufeira. Let the haunting melodies and soulful vocals transport you to another time and place as you savor authentic Algarvian cuisine and local wines. It's the perfect way to immerse yourself in the cultural heritage of the region before bidding farewell to the Algarve.

- Average Cost: Fado performance - $15-$25/£12-£20 per person, meals - $10-$15/£8-£12 per person

- Opening Hours: Fado performances typically start in the evening (check specific venue for details)

- Address: Various Fado houses in Albufeira, Algarve, Portugal

- Amenities: Reservations recommended, live music, traditional cuisine

As your budget-friendly journey through the Algarve comes to an end, take with you memories of sun-kissed beaches, rugged landscapes, and warm hospitality. Remember, the true beauty of travel lies not in the destinations we visit, but in the experiences we create along the way. Until next time, bom viagem!

Historical itinerary

Day 1: Journey Through Time

Welcome to Algarve, where history and culture intertwine to create a tapestry of captivating stories and ancient wonders. Embark on a journey through time as we explore the region's rich historical heritage.

Morning: Discover Faro's Historic Old Town

Begin your day in Faro, the capital of the Algarve, and immerse yourself in its centuries-old history. Start with a visit to the Faro Cathedral, a magnificent example of Gothic architecture dating back to the 13th century. Marvel at its ornate interiors, intricate carvings, and stunning views from the bell tower. Then, wander through the labyrinthine streets of the historic old town, where Moorish influences blend seamlessly with Portuguese charm. Admire the Arco da Vila, a triumphal arch that once marked the entrance to the medieval city, and explore the atmospheric alleys lined with traditional whitewashed houses and quaint cafes.

- Average Cost: Free (donations accepted at the cathedral)

- Opening Hours: Faro Cathedral - 9:30 AM to 5:30 PM (closed on Sundays)

- Address: Faro Cathedral, Largo da Sé, 8000-138 Faro, Portugal

- Contact: +351 289 806 898

- Amenities: Guided tours available, restrooms nearby

Afternoon: Journey to the Past in Tavira

In the afternoon, travel east to the charming town of Tavira, known for its rich history and well-preserved architectural gems. Explore the Tavira Castle, a Moorish fortress dating back to the 11th century, which offers panoramic views of the town and the Gilão River. Stroll along the Roman Bridge, one of the town's most iconic landmarks, and visit the Tavira Municipal Museum to learn more about the region's history, culture, and traditions.

- Average Cost: Castle admission - $3/£2.50, museum admission - $2/£1.50

- Opening Hours: Tavira Castle - 9:00 AM to 5:30 PM (closed on Mondays), Tavira Municipal Museum - 10:00 AM to 6:00 PM (closed on Mondays)

- Address: Tavira Castle, Rua da Galeria, 8800-307 Tavira, Portugal; Tavira Municipal Museum, Palácio da Galeria, Largo D. Paio Peres Correia, 8800-951 Tavira, Portugal

- Contact: Tavira Castle - +351 281 320 500, Tavira Municipal Museum - +351 281 320 500

- Amenities: Guided tours available at the castle, restroom facilities at the museum

Evening: Sunset at Castro Marim

As the day comes to a close, venture to the historic town of Castro Marim, nestled along the Guadiana River near the Spanish border. Explore the medieval Castro Marim Castle, which offers panoramic views of the surrounding countryside and the nearby salt flats. Don't miss the opportunity to witness a breathtaking sunset from this vantage point, casting a warm glow over the landscape and evoking a sense of wonder and tranquility.

- Average Cost: Free

- Opening Hours: Castro Marim Castle - 10:00 AM to 6:00 PM (closed on Mondays)

- Address: Castro Marim Castle, Rua 25 de Abril, 8950-138 Castro Marim, Portugal

- Contact: +351 281 531 800

- Amenities: Guided tours available, restrooms nearby

Day 2: Exploring Ancient Ruins

On the second day of your historical itinerary, delve deeper into the region's past with visits to ancient ruins and archaeological sites.

Morning: Roman Ruins of Milreu

Start your day with a visit to the Roman ruins of Milreu, located near the town of Estoi. Explore the remains of a luxurious Roman villa, complete with intricate mosaics, thermal baths, and a temple dedicated to the goddess Venus. Marvel at the craftsmanship of the ancient artisans and imagine life in Roman times as you wander through the well-preserved ruins.

- Average Cost: $3/£2.50

- Opening Hours: 10:00 AM to 5:00 PM (closed on Mondays)

- Address: Ruínas de Milreu, Sitio de Milreu, 8005-411 Estoi, Portugal

- Contact: +351 289 997 566

- Amenities: Guided tours available, restrooms nearby

- Afternoon: Moorish Legacy in Albufeira

In the afternoon, travel to the coastal town of Albufeira and discover its Moorish legacy at the Albufeira Castle. Perched atop a hill overlooking the old town, this medieval fortress offers panoramic views of the surrounding area and provides insight into the region's Moorish past. Explore the castle's ruins, wander through the charming streets of the old town, and soak up the atmosphere of this historic enclave.

- Average Cost: Free

- Opening Hours: Open all day

- Address: Albufeira Castle, Rua Henrique Calado, 8200-091 Albufeira, Portugal

- Amenities: Limited facilities, steep staircase to access castle ruins

Evening: Medieval Dinner in Silves

End your day with a taste of medieval life at a themed dinner in the historic town of Silves. Step back in time as you dine on traditional Portuguese cuisine served in a medieval setting, complete with period costumes, music, and entertainment. Immerse yourself in the ambiance of the Middle Ages and experience a truly unique culinary adventure.

- Average Cost: $20-$30/£15-£25 per person

- Opening Hours: Evening (reservation required)

- Address: Various venues in Silves, Algarve, Portugal

- Amenities: Reservations required, themed entertainment, traditional cuisine

Day 3: Maritime Heritage

On the final day of your historical itinerary, explore the maritime heritage of the Algarve with visits to coastal fortresses and maritime museums.

Morning: Fortaleza de Sagres

Begin your day at the Fortaleza de Sagres, a historic fortress located on the southwestern tip of the Algarve. Built in the 15th century by Prince Henry the Navigator, this imposing fortress played a crucial role in Portugal's Age of Discovery. Explore the fortifications, admire the panoramic views of the coastline, and learn about the region's maritime history at the onsite museum.

- Average Cost: $3/£2.50

- Opening Hours: 9:00 AM to 5:30 PM (closed on Mondays)

- Address: Fortaleza de Sagres, 8650-999 Sagres, Portugal

- Contact: +351 282 620 140

- Amenities: Guided tours available, restrooms onsite

Afternoon: Maritime Museum of Lagos

In the afternoon, journey to the coastal town of Lagos and visit the Maritime Museum, housed in the historic Governors' Castle overlooking the harbor. Delve into the maritime heritage of the Algarve through exhibits showcasing ancient navigational instruments, model ships, and artifacts recovered from shipwrecks. Gain insight into the region's seafaring traditions and the exploration of new worlds during the Age of Discovery.

- Average Cost: $2/£1.50

- Opening Hours: 10:00 AM to 6:00 PM (closed on Mondays)

- Address: Museu Municipal Dr. José Formosinho, Praça Infante Dom Henrique, 8600-763 Lagos, Portugal

- Contact: +351 282 770 000

- Amenities: Guided tours available, restrooms onsite

Art and culture itinerary

Day 1: Exploring Historic Landmarks

Morning:

Our first day begins with a journey back in time as we visit the historic landmarks that have shaped Algarve's cultural landscape. Start your day with a visit to the captivating Castle of Silves, perched majestically atop a hill overlooking the town of Silves. Dating back to the Moorish era, this imposing fortress offers breathtaking views of the surrounding countryside and a glimpse into Algarve's rich history. Explore the castle's well-preserved walls, towers, and ancient artifacts, and immerse yourself in the stories of battles and conquests that echo through its halls.

Castle of Silves:

- Address: Rua do Castelo, 8300-138 Silves, Portugal
- Phone: +351 282 440 839
- Opening Hours: 9:00 AM - 6:00 PM
- Admission Fee: $5/£4
- Amenities: Guided tours, gift shop

Afternoon:

After a morning steeped in history, continue your cultural journey with a visit to the charming town of Lagos. Wander through the cobblestone streets lined with colorful buildings adorned with traditional Portuguese tiles, known as azulejos. Make your way to the Slave Market Museum, housed in a former slave market dating back to the 15th century. Delve into the dark history of the transatlantic slave trade and gain insights into Portugal's colonial past through interactive exhibits and multimedia presentations.

Slave Market Museum:

- Address: Rua da Liberdade 279, 8600-660 Lagos, Portugal
- Phone: +351 282 764 734
- Opening Hours: 10:00 AM - 6:00 PM (Closed on Mondays)
- Admission Fee: $8/£6.50
- Amenities: Audio guides, educational programs

Evening:

As the day draws to a close, savor the flavors of Algarve with a dinner at a traditional Portuguese restaurant. Indulge in local specialties such as grilled sardines, cataplana (seafood stew), and pastéis de nata (custard tarts), accompanied by a glass of refreshing Vinho Verde or a robust red wine from the Algarve region. Let the warmth of Portuguese hospitality envelop you as you dine amidst the cozy ambiance of a family-run eatery, where every dish tells a story of tradition and taste.

Day 2: Immersing in Contemporary Art

Morning:

Wake up to a new day filled with artistic inspiration as we explore the thriving contemporary art scene of Algarve. Begin your morning with a visit to the Tavira Municipal Museum, housed in a beautifully restored 17th-century palace overlooking the Gilão River. Discover a diverse collection of modern and contemporary artworks by local and international artists, ranging from paintings and sculptures to installations and multimedia pieces. Be sure to check out the museum's rotating exhibitions, showcasing the latest trends and talents in the world of contemporary art.

Tavira Municipal Museum:

- Address: Palácio da Galeria, Largo D. Paio Peres Correia, 8800-951 Tavira, Portugal
- Phone: +351 281 320 500
- Opening Hours: 10:00 AM - 6:00 PM (Closed on Mondays)
- Admission Fee: $4/£3.50
- Amenities: Guided tours, art workshops

Afternoon:

Continue your artistic journey with a visit to the Algarve Center for Contemporary Art (Centro de Arte Contemporânea Algarve), located in the heart of Faro. Housed in a striking modern building, this dynamic cultural hub showcases cutting-edge works by emerging and established artists from Portugal and beyond. Explore the galleries filled with thought-provoking installations, avant-garde sculptures, and experimental multimedia artworks that challenge conventions and ignite the imagination. Don't miss the opportunity to engage with the local art community through workshops, lectures, and artist residencies hosted by the center.

Algarve Center for Contemporary Art:

- Address: Rua de São Francisco, 8000-462 Faro, Portugal
- Phone: +351 289 829 950
- Opening Hours: 10:00 AM - 7:00 PM (Closed on Mondays)
- Admission Fee: Free
- Amenities: Exhibition spaces, artist studios, library

Evening:

As night falls, immerse yourself in the vibrant cultural scene of Faro with a visit to one of the city's theaters or performance venues. From experimental theater and contemporary dance to classical music concerts and jazz performances, Faro offers a diverse array of cultural experiences to suit every taste. Catch a show at the Teatro Lethes, a historic theater dating back to the 19th century, or head to the Faro Municipal Theater for a night of world-class entertainment. Let the magic of live performance transport you to new realms of creativity and expression, as you celebrate the artistry of Algarve.

Teatro Lethes:

- Address: Rua de Portugal 17, 8000-281 Faro, Portugal
- Phone: +351 289 878 908
- Showtimes and Tickets: Available on website
- Amenities: Bar, cloakroom

Gastronomic Adventure

We'll delve deep into the culinary treasures of this enchanting region. From savoring fresh seafood by the sea to indulging in traditional delicacies in quaint villages, prepare your taste buds for an unforgettable journey.

Day 1: Coastal Culinary Delights

Morning: Start your day with a hearty breakfast at Café Fresco in Faro (Address: Rua de Portugal 14, Faro). This charming café offers a selection of freshly baked pastries, along with aromatic Portuguese coffee to kickstart your day.

After breakfast, head to Olhão, where you'll embark on a culinary journey through the famous Olhão Municipal Market

(Address: Largo da Restauração, Olhão). Here, you'll find an abundance of fresh seafood, colorful fruits, and aromatic spices. Take your time to wander through the market stalls, interacting with local vendors and sampling their delicious offerings.

Lunch: For lunch, indulge in a seafood feast at Restaurante A do João (Address: Avenida da República, Olhão). This family-owned restaurant is renowned for its grilled fish and seafood specialties, sourced directly from the nearby market. Be sure to try their famous cataplana, a traditional Algarvian seafood stew cooked in a copper pot.

Afternoon: After lunch, take a leisurely stroll along the Ria Formosa Natural Park (Address: Ria Formosa, Olhão). This stunning coastal lagoon is a haven for birdwatchers and nature lovers, with its diverse ecosystem of salt marshes, sand dunes, and lagoons. Explore the walking trails and keep an eye out for flamingos, herons, and other native bird species.

Evening: As the sun sets, head back to Faro and dine at Vila Adentro Restaurante (Address: Rua de São Francisco 18, Faro). This cozy restaurant tucked away in the historic Old Town serves up traditional Algarvian dishes with a modern twist. Sample their grilled octopus or cataplana de marisco, accompanied by a glass of local wine.

Day 2: Culinary Heritage in the Countryside

Morning: Rise and shine with a delicious breakfast at Casa do Campo (Address: Estrada Nacional 125, Almancil). This rustic farmhouse-turned-restaurant offers a farm-to-table dining experience, with fresh eggs, homemade bread, and organic produce sourced from their own gardens.

After breakfast, venture inland to the charming village of Alte, known for its picturesque setting and traditional Algarvian architecture. Explore the narrow cobblestone streets lined with whitewashed houses, and visit the Fonte Pequena (Address: Largo José Cavaco Vieira, Alte), a natural spring where locals gather to fill their water jugs.

Lunch: For lunch, dine at O Folclore (Address: Rua da Igreja, Alte), a quaint restaurant serving authentic Algarvian cuisine. Feast on hearty dishes such as cozido à portuguesa, a traditional Portuguese stew made with a variety of meats and vegetables, or cataplana de porco, a pork and clam stew cooked in a traditional copper pot.

Afternoon: After lunch, take a scenic drive through the rolling hills of the Algarve countryside, stopping at local farms and wineries along the way. Visit Quinta do Frances (Address: Estrada Nacional 124-1, Loulé), a family-owned winery where you can tour the vineyards and sample their award-winning wines.

Evening: Return to Almancil for dinner at A Quinta (Address: Rua do Comércio 4, Almancil), a charming restaurant housed in a restored farmhouse. Indulge in their seasonal tasting menu, featuring dishes inspired by the flavors of the Algarve countryside, paired with carefully selected local wines.

Day 3: Coastal Elegance and Fine Dining

Morning: Enjoy a leisurely breakfast at your accommodation, savoring the last moments of your gastronomic adventure in the Algarve. If you're staying in a luxury resort, take advantage of their buffet spread featuring an array of fresh fruits, pastries, and made-to-order omelets.

After breakfast, spend the morning exploring the picturesque town of Lagos. Wander through the cobbled streets of the historic Old Town, admiring the colorful tiled facades and ancient city walls. Don't miss the opportunity to visit the Mercado Municipal (Address: Rua General Alberto da Silveira, Lagos), a bustling market where you can pick up local cheeses, olives, and other gourmet treats.

Lunch: For your final meal in the Algarve, treat yourself to a fine dining experience at Restaurante Bon Bon (Address: Rua do Cerrinho, Carvoeiro). This Michelin-starred restaurant is renowned for its innovative cuisine and breathtaking ocean views. Indulge in their tasting menu, which showcases the best of Portuguese gastronomy with a modern twist.

Afternoon: After lunch, spend your final afternoon in the Algarve relaxing on the beach or exploring the rugged coastline. If you're feeling adventurous, book a boat tour to visit the famous Benagil Sea Cave (Address: Praia de Benagil, Lagoa), a stunning natural wonder with golden sands and crystal-clear waters.

Evening: As the sun sets on your Algarve adventure, reflect on your culinary journey over a glass of port wine at a waterfront café in Portimão. Savor the flavors of the region one last time, as you bid farewell to this enchanting corner of Portugal.

Nature and Parks Day

Day 1: Exploring Ria Formosa Natural Park

Morning:

As the sun rises over the Algarve, immerse yourself in the serene beauty of Ria Formosa Natural Park. This coastal gem spans over 18,000 hectares and is a haven for wildlife enthusiasts and nature lovers alike. Start your day by visiting the visitor center located at Quinta do Lago. Here, you can gather information about the park's diverse ecosystems, including marshes, lagoons, and barrier islands.

After acquainting yourself with the park, embark on a guided boat tour through its intricate network of waterways. Marvel at the rich biodiversity as you spot flamingos, herons, and other migratory birds that call Ria Formosa home. Don't forget to bring your camera to capture the breathtaking landscapes and colorful birdlife.

- Address: Quinta do Lago, 8135-024 Almancil, Portugal
- Contact: +351 289 843 108
- Opening Hours: 9:00 AM - 5:00 PM (Monday to Friday); 10:00 AM - 4:00 PM (Weekends)
- Website: www.icnf.pt/rea/parque-natural-da-ria-formosa
- Average Cost: $25-$40 per person for a guided boat tour

Afternoon:

After your boat tour, head to one of the picturesque islands within Ria Formosa for a relaxing afternoon on the beach. Ilha de Culatra and Ilha de Faro are popular choices, offering pristine sands and crystal-clear waters. Pack a picnic lunch or indulge in fresh seafood at one of the local beachside restaurants.

Spend the afternoon swimming, sunbathing, or simply strolling along the shoreline. If you're feeling adventurous, consider renting a kayak or paddleboard to explore the park's hidden coves and mangrove forests at your own pace.

Evening:

As the day draws to a close, make your way back to the mainland and treat yourself to a sumptuous seafood dinner at one of the nearby coastal towns. Olhão, known as the "capital of the Ria Formosa," boasts an array of waterfront restaurants serving up mouthwatering dishes like grilled sardines, octopus salad, and cataplana—a traditional Portuguese seafood stew.

After dinner, take a leisurely stroll along the harbor promenade and soak in the vibrant atmosphere as locals and tourists alike gather to enjoy the evening breeze. End your day with a nightcap at a cozy bar or café, where you can savor a glass of local wine or a refreshing gin and tonic.

Day 2: Exploring Costa Vicentina Natural Park

Morning:

On your second day in Algarve, venture westward to Costa Vicentina Natural Park, a rugged wilderness stretching along the region's Atlantic coast. Start your morning by driving to the park's northern entrance near the town of Odeceixe.

Once inside the park, lace up your hiking boots and hit the trails to explore its untamed beauty. The Rota Vicentina offers a network of well-marked hiking routes catering to all skill levels, from gentle coastal walks to challenging cliff-top treks. One of the park's highlights is the Fishermen's Trail, which winds its way along the coastline, offering breathtaking views of towering cliffs and hidden coves.

- Address: Parque Natural do Sudoeste Alentejano e Costa Vicentina, 7630-174 Odemira, Portugal
- Contact: +351 282 695 624
- Opening Hours: N/A
- Website: www.rotavicentina.com/en/

- Average Cost: Free for hiking; $10-$20 for guided tours (optional)

Afternoon:

After working up an appetite on the trails, head to one of the park's charming coastal villages for a traditional Portuguese lunch. Zambujeira do Mar and Vila Nova de Milfontes are both popular choices, offering a variety of cozy eateries serving up fresh seafood and regional specialties.

After lunch, spend the afternoon exploring the park's hidden gems, such as the stunning Praia do Amado—a favorite spot among surfers—or the picturesque village of Carrapateira, nestled amidst rolling hills and sandy dunes.

Evening:

As the sun begins to set, make your way to the coastal town of Aljezur, where you can savor a delicious dinner overlooking the ocean. Aljezur is known for its laid-back atmosphere and traditional Algarvian cuisine, with dishes like cataplana de marisco (seafood stew) and arroz de polvo (octopus rice) taking center stage.

After dinner, take a stroll through the town's cobbled streets and discover its hidden treasures, from ancient Moorish ruins to artisan shops selling locally made crafts. End your evening with a nightcap at a cozy bar, where you can mingle with locals and fellow travelers under the starry sky.

Day 3: Exploring Monchique Mountains

Morning:

On your final day in Algarve, escape the coastal crowds and head inland to the serene beauty of the Monchique Mountains. Start your morning by driving to the charming town of Monchique, nestled amidst lush forests and verdant hillsides.

Upon arrival, take some time to explore the town's historic center, with its whitewashed houses, cobblestone streets, and quaint cafes. Don't miss the opportunity to visit the Mercado Municipal, where you can sample local delicacies like honey, cheese, and cured meats.

- Address: Monchique, 8550-425 Monchique, Portugal
- Contact: +351 282 910 231
- Opening Hours: 8:00 AM - 2:00 PM (Monday to Saturday); Closed on Sundays
- Website: www.cm-monchique.pt/pt/mercado-municipal
- Average Cost: Free

Afternoon:

After exploring Monchique, venture deeper into the mountains to discover the region's natural wonders. One of the highlights is Caldas de Monchique, a spa town famed for its thermal waters and healing properties. Take a leisurely stroll through the lush botanical gardens or relax in the soothing thermal baths, rejuvenating both body and soul.

For those seeking adventure, the mountains offer a wealth of outdoor activities, from hiking and mountain biking to birdwatching and paragliding. Lace up your boots and hit the trails to explore hidden waterfalls, ancient forests, and panoramic viewpoints offering sweeping vistas of the Algarve coastline.

Evening:

As the day comes to an end, treat yourself to a hearty dinner at one of Monchique's traditional tavernas, where you can savor hearty mountain cuisine like feijoada (bean stew) and grilled meats. Pair your meal with a glass of local wine or a refreshing craft beer brewed in the nearby town of Silves.

After dinner, take a leisurely stroll through the town under the twinkling stars, soaking in the peaceful ambiance of this mountain retreat. Reflect on your adventures in Algarve as you savor the last moments of your journey, filled with memories of stunning landscapes, warm hospitality, and unforgettable experiences.

Music and Nightlife Excursion
Day 1: Immersive Cultural Experience

Start your Algarve adventure by immersing yourself in the vibrant culture and music scene of the region. Begin your day with a visit to Fado na Baixa, located at Rua do Moinho Velho, 10, Faro. This cozy Fado house offers authentic Portuguese cuisine and soul-stirring Fado performances. The melancholic melodies and heartfelt lyrics will transport you to the heart of Portuguese tradition. Make sure to arrive early to secure a good spot and enjoy a leisurely lunch accompanied by live music.

After lunch, take a stroll through the charming streets of Faro's historic center. Stop by the Cidade Velha, or Old Town, to admire the cobblestone alleys, whitewashed buildings, and picturesque squares. Don't miss the opportunity to explore Faro Cathedral, a stunning example of medieval architecture, located at Largo da Sé, Faro.

In the evening, head to R. de São Pedro, in Albufeira's Old Town, for a taste of Algarve's bustling nightlife. Start your evening with dinner at A Ruina, a popular restaurant offering delicious seafood and stunning views of the Albufeira coastline. After dinner, wander through the narrow streets lined with bars and clubs, such as Matt's Bar and Wild & Co., where you can dance the night away to live music or DJ sets.

Day 2: Beach Day and Sunset Serenade

Wake up early and embark on a scenic drive to Praia da Marinha, one of the most beautiful beaches in the Algarve. Spend the morning soaking up the sun, swimming in the crystal-clear waters, and exploring the rugged cliffs and hidden coves. Don't forget to pack a picnic to enjoy on the beach!

In the afternoon, head to Carvoeiro, a picturesque fishing village nestled between towering cliffs. Wander along the scenic coastal path to Algar Seco, a natural rock formation with stunning sea caves and blowholes. Take a boat tour to explore the caves up close and marvel at the breathtaking views of the coastline.

As the sun begins to set, make your way to Praia dos Pescadores in Albufeira. Join locals and visitors alike on the beach to watch the spectacular sunset over the Atlantic Ocean. Stay for the evening and enjoy live music and entertainment at one of the beachfront bars, such as Café Del Mar or NoSoloÁgua, where you can dance under the stars until the early hours of the morning.

Day 3: Wine Tasting and Cultural Exploration

Spend your final day in the Algarve exploring the region's rich cultural heritage and indulging in delicious food and wine.

Start your day with a visit to Quinta dos Vales, located in Estômbar, Lagoa. This family-owned winery offers guided tours and tastings of their award-winning wines, including traditional Portuguese varietals such as Touriga Nacional and Aragonez. Learn about the winemaking process and enjoy stunning views of the vineyards and surrounding countryside.

After your wine tasting experience, head to Silves, a historic town known for its Moorish castle and picturesque streets. Explore the narrow alleys and charming squares, and don't miss the opportunity to visit Silves Cathedral and the Municipal Market. For lunch, dine at Restaurante Marisqueira Rui, a local favorite known for its fresh seafood and traditional Portuguese dishes.

In the afternoon, take a leisurely drive along the N125, stopping at picturesque villages and scenic viewpoints along the way. Enjoy the breathtaking views of the Algarve countryside and coastline as you make your way back to your accommodation.

As night falls, head to Rua Vasco da Gama in Lagos for a taste of Algarve's vibrant nightlife. Start your evening with dinner at Restaurante Adega da Marina, where you can enjoy delicious Portuguese cuisine and local wines. After dinner, wander through the charming streets of Lagos' historic center, stopping at bars and clubs such as The Tavern and Inside Out, where you can dance the night away to live music or DJ sets.

End your Algarve adventure on a high note, savoring the memories of your music and nightlife excursion in this beautiful region of Portugal.

Family friendly itinerary

Day 1: Beach Fun and Water Activities

Kick off your family-friendly adventure in the Algarve with a day of beach fun and water activities. Head to Vilamoura Beach, where you can relax on the golden sands and take a dip in the calm, shallow waters of the Atlantic Ocean. Rent a pedalo or paddleboard and explore the coastline with your family, or join a guided boat tour to discover hidden caves and coves.

For lunch, grab a bite to eat at Tico Tico, a beachfront restaurant offering a diverse menu of fresh seafood, salads, and sandwiches. After lunch, treat your kids to some ice cream or gelato from one of the nearby kiosks before heading back to your accommodation for a relaxing afternoon by the pool.

In the evening, venture into Albufeira's Old Town for dinner and entertainment. Dine at Johnny Hooper's Saxophone Bistro, a family-friendly restaurant with a lively atmosphere and delicious food. After dinner, take a stroll along the bustling streets lined with souvenir shops and street performers, and don't miss the opportunity to catch a live music or magic show at The Strip.

Day 2: Nature Exploration and Wildlife Encounters

Start your day with a visit to Zoomarine, located in Guia, Albufeira. This family-friendly theme park offers a variety of educational and entertaining attractions, including dolphin shows, sealife presentations, and animal encounters. Watch in awe as dolphins perform acrobatic stunts and learn about marine conservation efforts from knowledgeable staff members.

After exploring Zoomarine, head to Parque Aventura Lagos, located in Lagos. This outdoor adventure park offers a range of activities suitable for all ages, including tree-top rope courses, zip lines, and climbing walls. Challenge your family to complete the various courses and enjoy stunning views of the surrounding countryside.

For lunch, picnic in the park or dine at Restaurante Parque Aventura, where you can enjoy a delicious meal while overlooking the adventure park. After lunch, explore the nearby nature trails and discover hidden caves and waterfalls before heading back to your accommodation for a well-deserved rest.

Day 3: Cultural Discovery and Family-Friendly Entertainment

Spend your final day in the Algarve exploring the region's rich cultural heritage and enjoying family-friendly entertainment. Start your day with a visit to Centro Ciência Viva do Algarve, located in Faro. This interactive science center offers hands-on exhibits and educational workshops designed to engage and inspire visitors of all ages. Learn about the wonders of the natural world and participate in fun experiments and demonstrations.

After exploring the science center, head to Ria Formosa Natural Park for a guided boat tour of the lagoon. Discover diverse ecosystems and observe native wildlife, including birds, fish, and crustaceans, as you navigate through the maze of channels and marshlands.

For lunch, dine at Restaurante O Costa, a family-friendly restaurant located in Faro's historic center, where you can enjoy traditional Portuguese cuisine and regional specialties. After lunch, explore the charming streets of Faro's Old Town, stopping to admire historic landmarks such as Faro Cathedral and Arco da Vila.

In the evening, head to Zoomarine for an unforgettable dinner and entertainment experience. Enjoy a delicious meal at one of the park's restaurants, followed by an evening performance featuring acrobats, dancers, and live music. End your family-friendly adventure in the Algarve with smiles on your faces and memories to last a lifetime.

Custom Travel Journal

Day 1 - [Date]:

"Travel is the art of knowing, and the canvas is the world. Paint your experiences with the colors of curiosity and the brushstrokes of awe."

Pre-Outing Reflections:

What are your expectations and hopes for today"s outing?
List one thing you want to learn or experience during your outing.

🌄 Morning Reflection:
Sunrise Thoughts: What thoughts or emotions did the sunrise evoke today?

🌍 Places Explored:
(List the notable places you visited today)

🍜 **Local Cuisine Tried:**
(Describe the local dishes you enjoyed and your thoughts on their flavors)

📷 Photo of the Day:
(Attach a memorable photo or sketch from your day)

✽ Memorable Moments:
(Highlight the most special moments of the day)

🌈 Unexpected Discoveries:
Hidden Gem Found: Describe a place or experience you stumbled upon unexpectedly.

Local Tradition Observed:
Share a unique local tradition or cultural aspect you observed today.

Cultural Insights:
Local Saying or Proverb: Include a saying or proverb you learned from a local and its meaning.

🌲 Nature Connection:
Nature's Impact: How did the natural surroundings contribute to your overall experience?

📝 Journaling Challenge:
Write a Postcard to Yourself: Draft a postcard to your future self-summarizing the day's adventures.

✿ Local Flora and Fauna:
Noteworthy Wildlife or Plants: Record any interesting wildlife or plant species encountered.

🐾 Navigation Triumphs:
Navigational Highlight: Share a successful navigation story or a challenge you overcame.

🌐 Global Connection:
Connect with Home: Describe how you stayed connected with friends or family back home today.

☾ Evening Contemplation:
Under the Stars: Reflect on the night sky or any stargazing experiences.

"As you collect memories in the scrapbook of your travels, remember that the most precious souvenirs are the lessons learned, the perspectives gained, and the growth cultivated."

Day 2 - [Date]

"The true alchemy of travel is the transformation of the ordinary into the extraordinary. May you find the extraordinary not only in the landscapes you explore but in the person you become."

Pre-Outing Reflections:
What are your expectations and hopes for today"s outing?
List two things you want to learn or experience during your outing.

⛰ Morning Exploration:
Early Adventures: Share your experiences and observations during the early morning hours.

🏰 Historical Encounters:
Historical Landmark Visited: Explore and document your visit to a historical site or landmark.

🥛 Local Beverages Tasted:
Sip of the Day: Describe any local beverages you tried and their flavors.

🌲 Nature Connection:
Nature's Tranquility: Reflect on a moment of tranquility in nature today.

🎬 Market Finds:
Market Treasures: List and describe unique items you discovered at local markets.

🎭 Cultural Immersion:
Cultural Performance or Art Encounter: Share your impressions of a cultural performance or art you witnessed.

Local Connections:
Memorable Encounter: Describe a meaningful interaction with a local resident.

🍽 Dinner Delights:
Dining Experience: Detail your dinner experience, including the ambiance and local flavors.

🌲 Outdoor Adventures:
Scenic Walk or Hike: Describe any outdoor activities, walks, or hikes you participated in today.

▰ Urban Exploration:
Cityscape Impressions: Share your thoughts on the urban landscape and any iconic city views.

🚗 Transportation Tales:
Unusual Transportation Experience: Describe any unique or interesting modes of transportation you used.

☀ Sunrise to Sunset:

Contrast of Day: Reflect on the differences between the sunrise and sunset experiences.

🌊 Waterfront Moments:
Waterfront Discovery: Share your impressions of any waterfront areas or activities.

🏰 Modern vs. Traditional:
Contrasting Architectural Styles: Compare and contrast modern and traditional architecture you encountered.

🛍 Souvenir Hunt:

Memorable Souvenir: Choose a souvenir that holds significance and explain its importance.

🎉 Local Celebrations:
Festive Atmosphere: Describe any local celebrations, events, or festivals happening today.

☐ Surprising Insights:
Unexpected Cultural Insight: Share a cultural nuance or insight that surprised you today.

📷 Capturing Moments:
Photo Challenge: Set a personal photo challenge for the day and share the results.

🎨 Nighttime Reflection:

Moonlit Thoughts: Reflect on how the night atmosphere influenced your mood.

"The world is a vast library, and each journey is a chapter. Write your story boldly, and may the lessons penned on the pages of your travels echo in your heart forever."

Day 3 - [Date]

"Exploration is not just a physical act; it's a spiritual odyssey. May your travels be a pilgrimage, leading you not only to new places but to the sacred chambers of your own growth."

Pre-Outing Reflections:
What are your expectations and hopes for today's outing?
List three things you want to learn or experience during your outing.

☀ Morning Serenity:

Nature's Awakening: Reflect on the serenity of the morning and any natural wonders witnessed.

🌲 Off the Beaten Path:
Hidden Trail Explored: Share your experiences exploring a less-known or hidden trail.

🍰 Culinary Adventures:
Dish of the Day: Highlight a local dish that stood out today and describe its preparation.

🎨 Artistic Encounters:
Local Artistic Expression: Discuss any local art or street art that caught your attention.

🌳 Nature Retreat:
Retreat to Nature:
Describe moments of solitude or relaxation in a natural setting.

♜ Historical Connections:
Personal Connection to History: Share any historical stories or events that personally resonated with you.

🚴‍♂ Active Pursuits:
Adventure Activity: Reflect on any adrenaline-pumping activities or adventurous pursuits.

🎞 Souvenir Stories:
Souvenir Symbolism: Explain the symbolism or memories associated with a chosen souvenir.

🎥 Sunset Reflection:
Sunset Contemplation: Reflect on the emotions and thoughts evoked during the sunset.

🌍 Cultural Exploration:
Cultural Workshop or Class: Describe any cultural workshops or classes you participated in today.

🚢 Water Adventures:
Water Excursion Highlights:
Share memorable moments from any boat rides, kayaking, or water excursions.

✿ Local Festivities:
Community Celebrations:
Reflect on any local celebrations or community events you joined.

🌲 Scenic Views:
Panoramic Views:
Describe the most breathtaking views you encountered today.

❊ Botanical Discoveries:
Botanical Garden or Nature Reserve:
Share experiences from exploring botanical gardens or natural reserves.

🎭 Theatrical Impressions:
Local Theater or Performance: Reflect on any theatrical performances or local shows attended.

Historic Pathways:
Historical Path Explored:
Discuss any historical pathways, streets, or districts explored.

🍹 Refreshing Beverages:

Local Refreshments:
Highlight refreshing local beverages sampled throughout the day.

☐ ♀ **Mindful Moments:**

Mindful Reflection:
Reflect on moments of mindfulness or tranquility experienced.

🎨 Nighttime Marvels:
Starry Night Impressions: Share your thoughts on the night sky and any celestial observations.

"In the footsteps of explorers, you find not only the imprints of their shoes but the imprints of their souls. Leave your mark on the world, and may the world leave its mark on you."

Printed in Great Britain
by Amazon